MORAL VALUES AND HIGHER EDUCATION

• A NOTION AT RISK •

MORAL VALUES AND HIGHER EDUCATION

• A NOTION AT RISK •

Edited by

Dennis L Thompson

Brigham Young University

LIBRARY OF CONGRESS CATALOGING-IN-PUBLICATION

Moral values and higher education: a notion at risk/edited by
Dennis L Thompson.
 179 p.   cm.
 Includes bibliographical references and index.
 ISBN 0-7914-0793-4. – ISBN 0-7914-0794-2 (pbk.)

 1. Moral education. 2. Education, Higher – Aims and objectives.
I. Thompson, Dennis L
LC283.M66   1990
378'.014 – dc20   90-19857
                                                           CIP

Distributed by State University of New York Press,
State University Plaza, Albany, New York 12446–0001

Contents

Contents

Contents

Acknowledgments

THIS VOLUME OF ESSAYS has been supported from the beginning by Jeffrey R. Holland. Through him the essays were commissioned under a grant from the office of the LDS Commissioner of Education. Numerous individuals were involved in discussions attempting to clarify the issues and frame the questions to be asked, including J. R. Kearl, Truman G. Madsen, Thomas J. Mathiesen, John J. Merrill, and C. Terry Warner. I received good counsel from George Bonham of the Palo Alto Medical Foundation and encouragement from Rene Girard of Stanford University.

We held a conference at Brigham Young University in which several of those mentioned above and most of the authors of the essays participated. This provided a foundation for discussion and understanding.

Jae R. Balliff, William E. Evenson, and Janet Y. Shiozawa provided unfailing support of the effort, and Howard A. Christy and Louise E. Williams edited the text and notes.

Academe — The Institutions and the Individuals: An Introduction to a Discussion of Morals in Higher Education

Dennis L Thompson

> *Give up money, give up fame, give up science, give up the earth itself and all it contains, rather than do an immoral act. And never suppose that in any possible situation, or under any circumstances, it is best for you to do a dishonorable thing, however slightly so it may appear to you.*
>
> — Thomas Jefferson

OVER A DECADE AGO Justice Blackmun said, "We have been and are in the midst of a wave of moral and ethical confusion. The balance has been missing. . . . We have retreated to discussions of situation ethics and of the 'new' morality, and we have rationalized and compromised and made excuses. And, of course, we continue to flounder."[1] More recently Barbara Tuchman observed—after recalling current events of cheating in the stock market, influence peddling, bureaucratic coverups, and corruption of elected officials—that public morality is mirrored in private morality and that the extent of public immorality becoming obvious to the average citizen is the ultimate disruption. Said she, "When I speak of disruption, I mean a period when we've lost belief in certain kinds of moral understanding of good and bad. . . . [People] don't know how to behave, they don't

Dennis L Thompson is an associate academic vice president at Brigham Young University.

know what's right and what's wrong."[2] The public has responded in much the same way. To the Gallup Poll question, "On the whole, would you say that you are satisfied or dissatisfied with the honesty and standards of behavior in this country today?" in 1986 two out of three answered that they were dissatisfied. (In 1973, 77 percent had been dissatisfied.[3]) This is merely a sample of many voices which have declared unease over the moral condition of contemporary society. Interestingly, this is not a phenomenon unique to the United States. Soviet literary journals, for example, have been flooded with articles decrying the moral degradation extant in the Soviet Union.

Universities have not excused themselves from this concern but have helped bring attention to it. In 1980 Steven Muller, president of Johns Hopkins University, conceded that "the biggest failing in higher eduction today is that we fall short in exposing students to values."[4] Jeffrey R. Holland, then president of Brigham Young University, in an address to the National Press Club in 1984, called the relegating of "moral and civic . . . values of education to the . . . back seat of the bus" a "notion" that has put our "nation at risk." A. Bartlett Giamatti, then president of Yale University, told the class of 1989 as freshmen that "a liberal education is training in how to discern those essential human values that make us free; it is training in how to express, in speech and writing, our commitment to those values in order to keep us free."[5] And Harold T. Shapiro, at his inaugural address in 1988 as president of Princeton University, appealed to American higher education to be more mindful of the moral and spiritual needs of college students. "We are better at research than at the public discourse required to transmit ideas and values," he said.[6]

Concern about the moral state of society runs from the fear of an obvious moral collapse to the welcome of personal freedom from constraints. In the middle, viewpoints of thoughtful commentators extend from a perceived decline in personal and social morality to an observation that we are a changing society with different needs and values from those of the past. In the first instance, some would argue that there is a set of values we can all agree upon which needs to be taught, promoted, or inculcated. These would probably include integrity, freedom, equality, and, perhaps, in America, pluralism and diversity. The set may also include both the value of tradition and the values of tradition and change—with the acknowledgment that they may conflict with each other. (Conflict between several of the above-mentioned values is often perceived; for example, freedom and equality have long been seen as unharmonious.) In the instance of the value of change, observers would not necessarily argue with any given value at any given time, but, in addition to pointing out the contradictions, would question how strongly the traditional values would be held when they come into conflict with something else—like tradition against progress, ambition against community, or careerism against professionalism.

Bruce Hafen argues in his essay that we have lowered our moral standards to meet the demands of reality and that we need to seek a balance between aspiration and reality. The extension of the "demands of reality" position is a pervasive situational ethic—seen not only in social relations and business, but in public life and religion as well. Adjustment is made to fit the occasion. In fact, it is often argued that society suffers from a surfeit of morality—with none being affected by it more than students—and that the proclaimed morality is often a superficial, unrealistic, or even hypocritical set of values—a morality which is always better for someone else than for oneself, one which deals with the surface of problems rather than the source.

Supporting this argument is the fact that, in real life, operational morality is too often not the same one which is proclaimed. The observable performance bears little relation to what has been asserted as the guiding morality—in business, the professions, politics, or education. Thus, there is a moral dualism—one for public assertion which we openly discuss and internally ascribe to, and another which governs performance and external relations. How one behaves within the company is on a different plane from what is permissible to achieve corporate goals. What is unaccepatable in our political candidates we may ignore in others with whom we agree in pursuing approval of common political goals. What the faculty demand of students in punctuality, originality, and understanding is not always returned in promptness, innovation, and clarity.

A continued concern for raising moral standards and an ongoing search for moral leadership essential to raising the standards is necessary. A lack of moral leadership is apparent not only in the university but in the government, the media, and elsewhere. Some institutions are even the sources of negative influences on society. Style becomes more important than substance, performance more respected than achievement. As James Billington argues, we become more concerned with the "aesthetics of power than with the content of policy."

We separate freedom from responsibility. A central concept of the nature of mankind is that individuals ought to be free. Freedom implies the right to make choices unencumbered by anyone else. That does not mean that the choices made are unfettered by consequences or conditions. While respecting one's freedom to make choices, we are not obligated to relieve him or her of the burden of resulting consequences—nor must we alter the conditions which impinge upon the circumstance. Thus, any instituation which is concerned with the moral imperatives must teach responsibility, for responsibility is the other side of morality. Someone must bear the responsibility for the consequences of choice. If we allow the choice to be made freely, then the responsibility must be assumed freely. To do otherwise is to denigrate the freedom of choice, for we alter the conditions in which the choice is made, therefore tipping the scale in favor of a choice without, or with reduced, consequences.

Must we agree on absolute moral imperatives to agree that there are some moral choices which are preferable to others? Can we assume that every opportunity for choice is a unique circumstance? We have moved into a societal condition where situation ethics reigns, where each choice "depends." Admittedly, situation ethics was introduced into a particular value structure of Christianity which, while decrying moral imperatives, insists that one value is superior to all the rest. Therefore, all further choices must be made in light of an omniscient standard. The most serious problem with that approach is that by introducing a sliding scale we introduce sliding scales. If everything can be adjusted we begin to adjust moral judgments for personal convenience. There are no longer standards for behavior; everything is negotiable. James Billington refers to this as relativism on norms, where equal value is ascribed to all norms. As the proclivity of man is toward comfort and convenience, we end up with decisions which produce the most gratification now.

One of my teachers, William Ebenstein, once said that that which is most moral is that which looks farthest into the future. In somewhat the same sense we end up paying for our moral credibility in the future. The more serious the breach the longer the payback period; witness Vietnam, where the wounds of the war continue to hurt.

If we deny moral imperatives we create excuses for our situational choices. Karl Menninger's book of several years ago, *Whatever Became of Sin?*[7] capsulizes the condition in which we find ourselves in the attitude that little or nothing is ever wrong. Sin is a judgment of moral insufficiency. If there is no outright moral error then there are only variants of approbation. Meg Greenfield wrote in her column, "We don't seem to have a word anymore for 'wrong' in the moral sense, as in, for example, 'theft' is 'wrong.' " We have developed alternatives to right and wrong which avoid moral judgment, she says, such as "right and stupid, right and necessarily unconstitutional, right and sick, right and only to be expected, and right and complex."[8] Often, in many instances, we don't even know what is right.

In the university we are put at a disadvantage because we debate in the abstract; we become a devil's advocate for pedagogical purposes; we can dismiss consequences for purposes of exploring processes. What we teach and learn heuristically must relate to a real world where there are real choices, real actions, and real results.

I do not doubt that we teach broadly the ethical consequences of choice—in the social sciences, the humanities, the professions. Why doesn't it stick? Is the object of the instruction too deeply ingrained in other standards of behavior? Do we not teach it enough? Is it rejected as inapplicable? Is it countered too often by obverse contentions? Does our performance belie our arguments? Probably some of all of that exists. The aggregate undermines our efforts.

Terrance Sandalow affirms that the university's only choice is to act morally in its relationships with its students. Again, in a Gallup Poll ranking of twenty-four professions on our perception of their honesty and ethical standards, college teachers tied for fourth, one of only six professions which rated above 50 percent.[9] Landrum Bolling once observed that the most influential people in a person's life have two qualities: they demand excellence and they care about the individual. It may be that on a personal level this is the best the university can ask of the faculty. But James Laney argues that faculty members do not want to be role models for the students, as the responsibility is too heavy. And Robert Coles illustrates the dilemma of a university being concerned with personal moral behavior when the students may have faced societal moral aberrations. To be involved is to stand disarmed in the task. The university must defend society and criticize it at the same time. To pursue ethical education would be to ask the university to promote a higher standard than is observed— perhaps to ask for more than it is willing to give. And there is always the concern that to enforce moral behavior implicitly teaches that moral values should be adhered to because they are backed by coercion, not because they are right.

There are different levels of morality and differences between them. Personal morality is different from social morality. They respond to different demands and different issues. Can the university be expected to influence and respond on both levels?

As late as the end of the last century the culminating course at many universities in this country was moral philosophy. The college president often personally taught the course to all senior students. It was intended to integrate the college experience and place it in an ethical context.[10]

Sandalow argues that the modern university operates under different conditions than it did in the nineteenth century. Today it has limited responsibilities to educate its students and to foster the advancement of knowledge. Yet the government and the students often look to the university to promote social justice, alumni and donors expect it to promote the common good, and parents often expect it to fill in where they have failed.

Warren Bryan Martin surveys the weaknesses of the university being looked to to provide moral understanding, and James Billington agrees that university administrators and faculty are neither responsible for the problem nor can they provide the remedies. Students come to the university as adults. The university or college cannot be held responsible for a regeneration of morality which has not been conveyed by schools, home, church, or the public institutions of society. It is neither at fault nor can it provide the solution. In fact, the university may be the least responsible for moral performance. The university is one of several participants in the mosaic of society—and only a portion of the others come into direct contact with it. Martin, again, for example, argues that it is the professional association which should set standards, not the university; and as the standards reflect specialties they are often devoid of values. Still, that does not excuse the university from contributing where it can—even if only in understanding the condition and the course of morality in the college. Billington believes that families and churches are not given adequate public support. Hafen also believes that parents and public schools need to be bolstered in their more basic task of moral preparation and that the universities can do that.

None of the authors really provide any prescriptions for developing a moral sense within the university. Some options remain open for discussion such as concern for the core. It is widely agreed that a common reading list creates a transforming experience when it is read. President Laney believes that it is not the curriculum, but the *ethos,* that is central to the university's contribution. Central to that, he argues, are the humanities. There is a perception that whatever binds people together has been lost, or at least has declined. This is what Robert Bellah and his associates have discussed as the loss of community and the rise of individualism.[11]

Abraham Kaplan does not believe that the university can inculcate values but rather that it can cultivate the "tools and resources for moral reflection." He refers to the university as providing an oasis for the life of the mind. While the university does not have a responsibility to teach morals, he says, it should teach ethics. In a like view, Ivana Marková discusses reflexivity—the ability to make reflexive judgments—as the moral element which requires monitoring and an area in which constant reflection on the world can take place. The university can provide this. Billington agrees that the role of the university is to train the critical intellect.

Sandalow does not believe that the university would be acceptable to impart values, nor that it has a record of being very influential. But this does not mean that it is irrelevant to the task. Its limited potential in one area does not mean that it cannot have an impact. It is, after all, a significant organization in society. That impact, he argues, can best be had by doing what the university does best—educating students. The university has a role in imparting a vision of what might be to its students, as well as training their minds.

Noel Reynolds would go further than any of the others in defining the responsibility of the university. He believes that the external relationship of the university to the community constitutes a moral responsibility to promote basic functions which are understood by both, while internal corporate responsibilities within the university translate into individual responsibilities for the various members of the academic community. Thus, institutionally and individually the corporate university is obliged to be engaged.

The debate on moral values and higher education will continue. These essays both focus our attention and widen our perspective. Significantly, they expand the discussion of the university's role in teaching moral behavior and performing moral duty.

Notes

1. Harry A. Blackmun, "Thoughts about Ethics," *Emory Law Journal* 24 (1975): 3:9.

2. Rushworth M. Kidder, "Barbara Tuchman," *The Christian Science Monitor,* Oct. 7, 1986, 19.

3. "Opinion Roundup," *Public Opinion* 9 (Nov./Dec. 1986): 22.

4. Quoted in Frank Goble and B. David Brooks, *The Cast for Character Education* (Ottawa, Ill.: Green Hill, 1983), 7.

5. A. Bartlett Giamatti, "A Liberal Education: The Values That Make Us Free," *The Atlantic Community Quarterly* (Winter 1985–86): 316.

6. "Call for Emphasis on Moral Values," *New York Times,* 9 Jan. 1988.

7. Karl A. Menninger, *Whatever Became of Sin?* (New York: Hawthorn Books, [1973]).

8. Meg Greenfield, "Why Nothing Is 'Wrong' Anymore," *Newsweek,* 28 July 1986, 72.

9. "Opinion Roundup," 21.

10. Douglas Sloan, ed., *Education and Values* (New York: Teachers College Press, Columbia University, 1980).

11. Robert N. Bellah et al., *Habits of the Heart* (Berkeley: University of California Press, 1985).

MORAL VALUES IN
HIGHER EDUCATION

1

Abraham Kaplan

WIDESPREAD IN OUR TIME is a spiritual hypochondria, a pervasive sense of imminent moral collapse. This is not so much a reaction to the moral complacency of an earlier time as it is the contemporary expression of old-fashioned parental anxiety and guilt. The medieval poet and philosopher Judah Halevi pointed out that the sin of the Golden Calf was committed by only one-half of one percent of the generation of the wilderness. Nowadays, there are many who speak of moral crisis as if today the numbers were reversed. They mistake every sound of a popgun for the crack of doom, as Emerson said of his contemporaries.

This generation is, no more than another, a generation of sinners. If there is a moral crisis today, it is less in people's whoring after false gods than in their not worshipping at all, being absorbed instead in narrow, immediate, and even petty concerns. It is a crisis of apathy, of moral indifference. Dostoevski's man from underground declares, "The world can go to pot as far as I'm concerned, so long as I get my glass of tea."

In personal terms, the crisis—if there is one—is embodied in the

Abraham Kaplan is a professor emeritus of philosophy and sociology at the University of Haifa.

tendency for each of us to go his own way: nationally, in the welter of special interests swamping concern for the general welfare; internationally, in self-seeking isolationism presenting itself as the pursuit of peace.

The apathy of our time is not new; what is new is only how much we now know to be indifferent to. Our unwillingness to be involved is much the same as in earlier times; "no man is an island," after all, is the theme of a seventeenth-century sermon. An earlier preacher than John Donne, by some two thousand years, admonishes, "If you say, It is no concern of mine, will not He who weighs men's hearts take note of it?" The notion that we can acquit ourselves of moral responsibility simply by disclaiming it is as old as Cain.

The Talmud points out that a myrtle can stand among thorns and remain a myrtle, but moral education cannot rise much higher than its source in the society of which the school is a part. The focus on higher education on behalf of moral values is misdirected—"they that are whole have no need of the physician, but they that are sick." It is society that is sick. With Thomas Jefferson, "I tremble for my country when I reflect that God is just."

In the political arena, government by consent often replaces force only by fraud, as it manipulates opinion; human rights are systematically denied in many countries; terror, torture, and assassination are widely accepted as instruments of policy; preparations for biological and nuclear warfare are extensive and accelerating.

On the social scene, sexism, racism, and ethnic and religious discrimination in one form or another are worldwide; child abuse gives crimes of violence an especially heinous cast; patterns of sexual conduct pose threats to the body as well as to the spirit.

In the marketplace, competitive waste and conspicuous consumption often serve as norms; production of drugs and other noxious substances enjoys the supports of a number of governments; price bears less relationship to worth than to wiles of marketing. We spend on advertising, in direct costs alone, three times as much as we do on higher education; the commodities advertised are chiefly cigarettes, junk foods, liquors, and cosmetics. For every dollar spent by the thirty-five top advertisers, the thirty-five top university libraries spend one and a half cents.

The ideal of equality has little bearing on radically unequal living standards, where there is a total lack of what Aristotle called distributive justice. Fewer than 10 percent of the American people own more than do the remaining 90 percent; one American in seven lives below the poverty level. Of the world population 70 percent is in poverty-stricken countries. Per capita income in the twenty richest countries is more than fifty times as great as in the twenty poorest countries, where the average income is $200 a year. No amount of higher learning will persuade students to take seriously ideals which are of little account to anyone else.

The situation with regard to commutative justice—what was done to deserve a good—contrasts even more starkly with pretended social values. We pay a hundred times as much to glamour girls, rock stars, and ball players as we pay to nurses, schoolteachers, and policemen. In the world of nations, income has nothing to do with either hard work or efficiency. In per capita income the United Arab Emirates and Kuwait rank first and fourth, while France and the United Kingdom are twelfth and sixteenth.

If higher education must do something about moral values, it is not to promote standards disregarded everywhere outside the classroom. It is, rather, in John Dewey's terms, to replace customary morality by reflective morality. In a university, moral education is essentially the acquisition and cultivation of materials, tools, and skills for moral reflection.

The values in customary morality may be the very ones to which reflection leads. Customary and reflective morality are distinct in their methods, but not necessarily in their contents. The intellectual quality of education lies in its readiness to bring convention before the bar of reason, not in its defiance of convention. Rebellion is no more than conformity in reverse.

The sophists who argued that morality is merely a matter of convention were only defining customary morality. There, moral norms are based—whatever their claims in theory—on the force of habit, on social sanctions, on peer-group pressures, and on the weight of authority. Customary morality is sustained by the quest for certainty and by the desire to escape from freedom, so that moral choices will evoke no anxiety beforehand and no guilt afterwards.

The moral education provided by customary morality dishes up canned thought and fresh-frozen opinions: just thaw, add water, and serve. A more fitting comparison might be with microwave cooking: customary morality provides in a few minutes what reflective morality can accomplish only after protracted and often agonizing reappraisal. For customary morality, there is no wrestling with the angel in the dark night of the soul. The hackneyed sermons denouncing sin provided by customary morality do not acquire academic standing by being recast into pedantic lectures.

When customary morality is applied, it is embedded in a pervasive dualism: facts and values, the one for weekdays and the other for Sundays; an objective world of action and a subjective world of feelings; one's professional life and one's personal life; harsh actualities and tender sentiments. Often, conventional definitions of masculine and feminine roles in society correspond to the two components of the dualism.

Such a dualistic outlook deprives reality of aspiration to the ideal, while ideals are left without any purchase on reality. They continue to be promulgated, but with no expectation that they will significantly affect action. Customary morality is a tyranny tempered by hypocrisy. Its ideals are high, but in practice its cardinal virtue is prudence. The sum of all its commandments is: Thou shalt not get caught! For this vulgar pragmatism, virtue always triumphs, because triumph is seen as the supreme virtue.

Moral values are not served by preachments, resolutions, and other devices of symbol magic. Required courses in philosophy would be as futile as compulsory attendance at chapel, if these are debased into promotions of customary morality—just as singing the national anthem at ball games scarcely engenders civic spirit and a genuine love of country.

Symbols, being abstractions, are no more than magical when they are cut off from concrete resources for action and concrete constraints on action. It is the absence of any linkage to such concreteness that makes appeals to character and backbone so ineffective. Freud once brought to his seminar a cartoon showing a country bumpkin in a hotel room trying to put out the newfangled electric light at his bedside by blowing on it. "You see, gentlemen," Freud then said to his students, "it is necessary to find the switch." One might say that to professors as well, if they mean to teach moral values. The task of higher education is to find switches, not to blow hard.

Customary morality, with its Brotherhood Weeks and Peace Marches, believes in the magic of symbols, taking ringing declarations and moral pronouncements to be themselves the solutions to moral problems. Pointing the way to solutions is not the same as being on our way; we leave off where we should begin. There is little to expect from extending to the venue of higher education what has achieved so little elsewhere.

The contents of reflective and customary morality may largely coincide, but there are certain respects in which they will almost surely differ. For one thing, customary morality often trivializes moral values. The good becomes the goody-goody; perceived "materialism" is countered by an emphasis on what is in fact immaterial, like codes of dress, hairstyles, and speech. The place of moral values in higher education is not filled by insistence on observance of the trivia of manners.

Customary morality often has a negative cast; it is preoccupied with vices rather than with virtues. Its motto seems to be that of Billie Dawn in *Born Yesterday:* "This country and its institutions belong to the people who inhibit it." Morality is far more than a set of prohibitions. In practice, customary morality enjoins, "Stay out of trouble," "Don't make waves," "Don't volunteer for anything," rather than such positive injunctions as "Love thy neighbor" and "Seek peace and pursue it." It is more concerned that public servants have negative virtues like temperance than that they make positive commitments to the public good and act on them.

Customary morality measures the morality of policy by the moral stature of the policymaker. Unfortunately, great and good men are quite capable of doing great wrong—that good intentions are not enough is deservedly notorious. Corruption is odious even when law does not recognize its existence. Society is even more depraved when immoral policy is socially accepted and institutionalized, as it has been in Nazi Germany, South Africa, and the Soviet Union.

The content of customary morality suffers from formalism as well as from legalism. Customary morality usually localizes moral issues only at the edges of policy rather than at its center, in the procedures of forming and implementing policy, not in what the policy is. To be sure, how a decision was made is sometimes more important than what was decided—sometimes, but not always. For customary morality, moral assessment seems to be based on the principle, "It ain't what you do, it's how you do it." Business ethics, for instance, is thought of as a matter of avoidance of bribery and kickbacks, unfair competition and false advertising, milking the corporation and trading on inside information. Moral values are equally at stake in practices conventionally accepted till yesterday, like discriminating against women and minorities, or still accepted today, like selling worthless and even harmful commodities such as quack medicines and tobacco.

The university has its own customary morality, one which endorses the dualism of fact and value, and assigns to higher education a concern only with the domain of fact. Neutralism in education is seen as the only alternative to indoctrination. Plato supposed that the Good need only be known to be desired, as the poet says of his beloved, "But to see her was to love her,/ Love but her, and love for ever." The prevailing modern view is that virtue is not knowledge but a desire for the Good beyond the knowing of it, perhaps without knowledge of it, or maybe even a desire for it in spite of what we know.

At issue is the conception of objectivity as detachment, of understanding as indifference, being uncaring or at least maintaining a balanced posture regardless of what we care about. This conception confuses a readiness to accept unpleasant truths supported by the evidence, which objectivity does require, with the notion that we are not objective if we care one way or another about our findings—as though medical research, for instance, is not objective if it values health more than the disease it seeks to eradicate.

Neutralism implies factualism. It allows values to enter into consideration only as subjects of neutral examination, to determine what people in fact value but not what they *should* value. At most, neutralism gives values a place with regard to the intellectual virtues. These, however, implicate and are implicated by the moral virtues. The passion for truth is, after all, a passion. Integrity, caution, and courage are as essential to the scientific enterprise as to moral aspiration.

If in our teaching we disregard moral values or tacitly cast a slur on them, we cannot expect that they will be conspicuously displayed in action. Customary academic morality is quite willing to teach values in the appreciation of art, literature, and music, or in the pursuit of excellence on the athletic field, but recoils from anything that smacks of teaching an appreciation of the greatness of the human spirit, and the pursuit of excellence in the human heart.

Our time is in the grip of what Bertrand Russell called subjectivist madness, for which not only values but even facts are thought to be subjectively determined. Over and over the question is raised, Who is to decide?—*who*, rather than *how* issues are to be decided. The implication is that whether a decision about values, at any rate, is right, depends only on how you look at it, which in turn is a matter of who is doing the looking. One person's point of view has as much claim to being right as another's—which is to say, as little claim. "There is nothing either good or bad, but thinking makes it so."

The quality of the thought escapes assessment, because there is nothing outside the thought by which to make the assessment, save another person's thought. For subjectivism, even one's own thought may not be involved. What signifies is not a thought but a feeling, not a belief but an attitude. The subjectivist position is that there is no arguing about tastes because argument aims at establishing a conclusion, and there is no conclusion to be reached when there is no process of deliberation to start with.

If taste is meant literally, the notion that no one's taste is better than anyone else's would startle wine connoisseurs and tea fanciers. Such a notion would also stultify any aspiration to cultivate one's own taste, for the effort is meant to improve taste, not just to change it. What can I mean by improving my taste if the only standard of worth I acknowledge is the taste I now have? Cultivation of taste may be difficult; it is surely not self-contradictory. The very idea of taste embodies a judgment of worth—to have taste is to like intuitively what considered judgment would appraise as worthy of being liked.

Judgment stops short at qualities of immediately given experience, what Clarence I. Lewis calls "intrinsic value." A would-be gourmet might acknowledge that he ought to prefer caviar to salted peanuts and bearnaise to ketchup, but gastronomic arguments will not change his actual preferences unless they change what in fact he experiences. I know of no moral issues, however, that hinge on immediately experienced quality. The morality of capital punishment, say, is not to be decided equally by the experience of victims, murderers, and executioners alike. It is the nadir of moral decadence to hold in all seriousness that sadism and child abuse, enslavement and torture, genocide and terror are no more than matters of taste—like a preference for chocolate or vanilla, only more intense.

The cultural relativism revealed by nineteenth-century ethnology produced a shock from which the Western world has not yet recovered. "There are people who honor madmen as prophets," said Heinrich Heine; "we look on prophets as madmen." For the relativist, false prophets are to be known, not by their fruits, but only by the knower's cultural identity or ideological identification.

Nowadays relativism is often called institutionalism or conventionalism, especially in aesthetics. The position is that if beauty is not in the eye of the beholder, this is only because the beholder is just an individual. The worth of a work of art is determined, not by the taste of any one person, but by the community of art lovers, or by institutions like Church and State. The art critic serves merely as their spokesman—if, indeed, he is not speaking only for himself. The same position is taken with regard to judgments of moral worth.

Subjective relativism attained respectability in twentieth-century philosophy as the doctrine of emotivism—that value judgments are not propositions capable of being true and false but, rather, expressions with the logic of interjections and imperatives. Emotivism holds that value judgments embody attitudes rather than beliefs; their substance is not thought but feeling; they arise from and appeal to emotions, not reason.

Yet emotions are not self-validating. They can be appropriate or inappropriate, evoked by well-founded understanding of the situation or by ignorance, error, and illusion. It is one thing to feel fear when confronted by a cobra and quite another to be afraid of a garden snake. Fear is rational if it is a response to real danger, and that is something which can be determined objectively. Why should we suppose that emotions involved in moral judgment are somehow exempt from comparable rational scrutiny? The heart has its reasons which reason does not know, but this is only to say that the reasons for our feelings may be hidden even from ourselves.

Value judgments can be given objective validation because they purport to characterize an external reality. Values are indeed relative to circumstances, but this alone does not deny them objectivity; it only implies that the value judgment must specify the circumstances relative to which the judgment is being made. That one man's meat is another man's poison does not make biochemistry subjective.

A person arriving at a value judgment may be relying on his own experience or he may know better, recognizing that his personal experience is limited, uninformed, or distorted. Whether his experience has a certain quality is not at issue; the judgment is attributing something to its own subject matter, not to the person judging. The argument that being of value (being right or good or their opposites) is not an attribute not only begs the question but is also beside the point. The issue is always what empirical attributes the subject of the judgment really has, in the relevant circumstances.

Emotivism takes its stand on the tenet that value conclusions cannot be derived from purely factual premises. That is true; objectivist ethics, however, does not smuggle values into its premises—emotivism smuggles values out. There always are values among our premises. No thought takes its departure from data to which it is wholly indifferent. We think only so as to remold reality nearer to the heart's desire (though the desire may be just to make reality more intelligible). There are no purely factual premises, unless premises are restricted to suit one or another tendentious formulation of the problem.

Valuation reaches out to a reality which already incorporates values. No value is self-contained, not only because of its external reference but also because it is always a component of a value system. More is always relevant than is defined by any given context. There is never only one value at stake; in the polity of ends there are no single-issue campaigns. Values are systemic, though they are not necessarily systematic. They may be disordered and inconsistent, but they are never alone.

Any particular value must be assessed by its consequences for other values. Infantilism cannot see beyond the immediate present; in various pathologies some single value becomes all-consuming. Moral judgment takes into account whatever values empirical interconnections make relevant. Reflection is called for because there is no telling *a priori* how a decision ostensibly about a particular value will affect the whole system of values of which the one in question is a part.

The polar antithesis to subjectivism is absolutism. The former holds that there can be no objective knowledge of what is right and good; the latter, that there is not only such knowledge but even certitude: unequivocal, unqualified, and incontrovertible moral truth. Today, subjectivism and absolutism seem to be dividing the world between them, ideologically speaking; the domain of objective relativism is minuscule by comparison.

The two extremes, like so many others, meet in the end: subjectivist and absolutist agree that the fundamental issue is always who is to decide. In subjectivism, each person decides as he sees fit; in absolutism, the decision is made by the appropriate authority. What we are to do is a foregone conclusion. The chestnut is, "You go your way; I'll go God's."

Absolutism is rarely so permissive. "We are not here to tolerate, but to extinguish falsehoods, put an end to them," Thomas Carlyle declared. That sense of mission takes it for granted that we already know which are the falsehoods. The assumption of infallible foreknowledge is the essence of absolutism. A religionist might recognize in the assumption the sin of self-righteousness, of spiritual pride. He might also recognize that his mission is not to lead the blind but to remove blindfolds, as the Hassidic master, Simchah Bunam, put it. In education, absolutism is doubly defeating: we cannot teach those who think they already know; and if it is the teacher who is an absolutist, no one is learning.

Moral certitudes are hard to come by because moral quandaries so often confront us with dilemmas. For the child, being good means only controlling impulse; for the adolescent, morality is still largely a matter of resolving conflicts between duty and desire. In maturity, moral issues are also posed by conflicting duties. We have duties to family and to friends; to our professions and those we serve and work for; to political groups and parties; to the state and whole peoples; to the human family and all that lies beyond; to future generations.

Morality is seldom the application of known solutions to already formulated problems. To identify the moral issues in a quandary is by no means always easy. Resolving the issues may be a task which would tax the inner resources of a saint and sage combined.

Clarity of moral principle can serve to cover up the ambiguity of moral practice. Even when ends are unequivocally moral, absolutism does not shrink from pursuing them by immoral means. Bodger's whisky and Undershaft's cannons will keep open the shelters for the homeless, Major Barbara is told. If ends are seen as absolute—worthy regardless of their conditions or consequences—then moral assessment of the means is irrelevant. Absolutism does not argue that the ends justify the means; it argues that means simply are in no need of moral justification.

Absolute ends define unalterable priorities. The ends are recurrently betrayed by their fixity in a world of flux. From unqualified goals we are forever driven by force of circumstance. The repetition in "Justice, justice shalt thou pursue," a commentator explains, is to enjoin justice in our means as well as in our ends. Means are subject to moral assessment because the means used in the pursuit of any one value implicate the whole system of values embodied in all our pursuits.

Assessments of both ends and means must be made over and over again—not once for all, as absolutism supposes. To the problems of life there are no answers in the back of the book, Kierkegaard remarked. Truth, whether of fact or of value, cannot be defined beforehand by its content, but only by the method by which it was attained—reflection on experience. True and false prophets both proclaim, "Thus saith the Lord"; they differ only in their fruits.

Science, said the physicist J. J. Thomson, is a policy, not a creed. That is one of the important differences between morality and religion. It also differentiates education from instruction, the transmission of what is taken to be true belief. For instruction, there *are* answers in the back of the book. Education is not concerned with storing and retrieving already processed data, but with acquiring, processing, and using new data. Education in chemistry, say, is a matter of teaching, not chemistry, but how to be a chemist. Moral education, certainly in higher education, goes beyond the moral instruction in childhood. It teaches, not morality, but how to be a responsible, reflective moral agent.

Moral absolutes generate nonnegotiable demands. They allow issues to be resolved only by the appeal to force, or to some other form of unreason. This is why they have no place in education. Pressure groups continually threaten the integrity of the educational process, each on behalf of its own absolutes. On the political scene, absolutists rely on propaganda, brainwashing, and thought control—from censorship to incarceration in mental hospitals. The most tyrannical governments, said Spinoza, are those which make crimes of opinions. Those would also be the most benighted institutions of learning.

All this is not to deny that there are *relative* absolutes, whether of fact or of value, so well established in such a wide range of contexts that they function as absolutes, as scientific or moral principles. The scientist unhesitatingly relies on the principles of conservation of angular momentum and of mass-energy. In the domain of value, the ideas that love is better than hate, peace better than war, and brotherhood better than bigotry are as nearly absolute as principles can be. For Jews, incest, murder, and idolatry are immoralities which they must eschew even at the cost of their lives. Other religions equally have their supreme values and their martyrs. Yet even truth, though mighty above all things, must sometimes give way, Hillel observed, as when we compliment a bride.

In the Western world, morality is widely thought to rest only on a religious basis. This may be true for Judaism, Christianity, and Islam; it is not true for Hinduism, Buddhism, and Taoism, for all of which morality is prerequisite to religion, rather than a derivation from religion. Even in the Western religions there are many who hold, not that an act is right because God enjoins it, but that He enjoins it because it is right. When Abraham pleads, "Shall not the Judge of all the earth do justly?" he is not asking for a tautology in reply.

Whatever the logic of the relation between religion and morality, the psychology is something else. In his "Dover Beach," Matthew Arnold laments that the sea of faith has ebbed. Morality was scarcely triumphant when the sea was at the full. Throughout history and into our own day so-called faith had its crusades and inquisitions, witch-hunts and religious wars, persecutions, pogroms, and genocides.

All of these have been condemned in religious teaching but what passes for religion is another matter. Spinoza's charge that faith has become "a mere compound of credulity and prejudice" expresses the view of countless religious teachers from the time of the prophets onward. In our own day T. S. Eliot has commented that "our literature is a substitute for religion, and so is our religion." Our time has its own idolatry. We have set foot on the moon, but astrology is as popular as ever; we have cracked the genetic code, but microbiology leaves nostrums and food fads untouched; we have explored the depths of the psyche, but gurus of occult meditation treat many more people than psychiatrists do.

The business of education, as of religious teaching, is to destroy idols, whose worship defies both reason and experience. Faith, said Kierkegaard, is not "a school for numbskulls, an asylum for the feeble-minded." To provide a place for moral values in higher education does not imply turning the university into such a school or asylum. Moral values do demand faith, but faith *in* the values, not faith *that* something or other is the case. What is called for is commitment, trust, and hope, not a substitute for reason. Tutelage in any substitute for reason only counterfeits education.

Moral norms must be internalized, or they lose their moral quality. When internalized, they make up conscience, the thrust of which is usually negative and punitive, directing action largely by anxiety and guilt. Left to itself, conscience is a wholly unreliable guide to action. The moral laws it enjoins it accepts without reflection, so that it does not transcend customary morality even though its dictates may be contrary to conventional standards. Moral education calls as much for a critique of conscience as for its strengthening.

The unreliability of conscience is revealed by the variability of its dictates. Conscience, if God-given, Freud noted, is an uneven and careless piece of work. Descartes once remarked that of all good things in the world, good sense is the most fairly distributed, because each of us is satisfied with his own share. On this criterion, conscience is the least fairly distributed, for most of us feel that we ourselves have too much while others have too little. One person's conscience permits actions which the conscience of another finds morally abhorrent. Because of such differences, the rule of conscience drives us once more into either subjectivism or absolutism.

Widespread in our time is the effort to persuade ourselves that there really are no differences in moral norms. A popular tactic is to suppose that we all agree in our ends and differ only in the means we choose to attain them. This might be called the eudaemonian theory, from Aristotle's term for the "happiness" to which everyone supposedly aspires. Unless such an allegedly common end is defined so broadly as to be empty, it is seldom common in fact. At issue is always what specific means are to be employed for the supposedly common end; differences here are real and important.

Another popular tactic is to invoke the precious essence theory, that differences are superficial and unimportant compared with underlying samenesses. This is hardly true of languages, family patterns, art styles, or political practices; why should we assume it to be true of moral codes? All that different soups have in common is water; the flavor, taste, and texture lie in what differentiates them from one another.

A third tactic is the spurious ecumenism which rests on what might be called the missing ingredient theory. Your religion, morality, or whatever is all very well in its way, the theory runs, but it would be vastly improved if it incorporated some of mine. Mine, in turn, lacks something important which only yours can give. In this way, it is hoped, differences will be reduced and ultimately disappear, to the advantage of all concerned. Such eclecticism and syncretism, pursued on behalf of an ideal of homogenized goodness, constitute a cowardly evasion of moral responsibility and a surrender of moral autonomy. The so-called Chanukkah bush honors neither the birth of Jesus nor the heroism of the Maccabees.

The basic moral problem of our time is not how to destroy differences but how to transcend them, how to achieve community without imposing uniformity. Here education has an important part to play. "Man is a tame animal," Plato observed; "nevertheless he requires proper education. If he is insufficiently or badly educated he is the most savage of earthly creatures." "The state," Aristotle agreed, "is a plurality which should be united and made into a community by education."

Transforming a plurality into a community without imposing uniformity defines pluralism. This is more than tolerance, which implies inferiority and indifference—letting others live, instead of living together with them. Pluralism means acceptance, living together even in the absence of agreement. I accept your values without abandoning or compromising my own when I recognize that yours are different from mine, acknowledge that you are nevertheless entitled to have them, and respect and cherish you for what you are rather than for what I can make of you. In a pluralistic society, if moral education is not pluralistic it has no place in public education, higher or not.

Even in a pluralistic society there are limits to acceptability—pluralism does not mean that anything goes. I can accept many cuisines but not cannibalism; many sex patterns but not child molesting and sadism; many political parties but not neo-Nazis and terrorists; many religions but not Satanism and human sacrifice. I myself may be the one who is not accepted. There are societies where whole ethnic groups are kept in the community but are not allowed to be of it, like blacks in South Africa and Jews in the Soviet Union. Community is not identity; it is living with differences, in equality and fraternity.

There are those for whom pluralism in the domain of values means that you pay your money and you take your choice. The cost is always real but the choice is not if it remains on the level of customary morality, letting others choose for us. The will, as Kant amplified, is not moral unless it is autonomous, making its own decisions. In Spinoza's terms, the moral agent is active rather than passive; we are moral only in so far as we understand what we are doing, and do it because of our understanding.

Morality presupposes freedom; that, in turn, presupposes knowledge. The values we pursue are not truly being chosen if we do not know their conditions and consequences. This is where education comes in. The Victorian injunction, "Be good, sweet maid, and let who will be clever" fails to recognize that one must be clever in order to know what is good in particular concrete circumstances. Moral aspiration is thwarted, not only by scoundrels, but even more by deluded fanatics and well-meaning fools.

Customary morality is not so much irrational as unthinking. One often hears that the moral life demands nothing more than obedience to the Ten Commandments. Among thousands of American students, I have found very few in public universities who could specify all ten. Everyone remembers the prohibition of adultery and murder, but hardly anyone recalls the injunction against bearing false witness. Only a few more remember the commandment to honor father and mother and the prohibition of stealing. "Thou shalt not covet," if remembered at all, is thought of only with reference to the neighbor's wife.

Traditional morality must be reinterpreted continually in order to be applicable to new circumstances. Such reinterpretation is the starting point of reflective morality. "False witness" acquires new meaning in a world of advertising and propaganda, of political image making, and of news managed as mass-media entertainment. "Love thy neighbor" has new implications in a time when, given the average density of urban life today, each of us has twenty thousand neighbors living within one mile. "Thou shalt not kill" must be made specific anew in relation to preemptive strikes, genetic engineering and organ transplants, life-support systems, and contraception.

What tradition once acknowledged as duties, like serving the feudal overlord, are now seen as impositions on freedom, while new duties, like safeguarding the environment and protecting endangered species, are emerging. Former rights, like establishing monopolies, are now seen as privileges, and former luxuries, like education, are now insisted on as necessities. Inequalities once accepted as fixities of a natural order of things are now recognized as inequities which can and ought to be corrected.

Whenever social patterns are redefined, new forms are likely to be condemned by traditionalists as destroying the values formerly attained in the church, the family, the state, the economy, and in other institutional frames. The need for new patterns in value pursuits in a rapidly changing world is what makes so futile the exhortation to return to the old-fashioned virtues. The credibility gap between the generations is greatest in the domain of customary morality.

The young lack neither aspiration to the moral life nor capacity for it; they lack only experience, and the knowledge and understanding that experience yields. When we confuse virtue with innocence, we deny the young the fruits of our own experience, except by way of producing in the young an unthinking conditioning. The tenet of customary morality that one cannot reason about moral teachings but simply obey them has been challenged since Socrates, who replaced it with the dictum that the unexamined life is not worth living. If values are exempt from rational assessment, they are left to habit, to caprice, or to manipulation by power elites.

Even the young have been caught up in the anti-intellectualism of our time. Starting with protests against dehumanizing uses of technology, anti-intellectualism moved on to hostility to technology as such, then to repudiation of science because it is the basis of technology, and finally to attacks on the intellect itself, as the progenitor of science. Here protestors and Establishment are at one, united in derogation of the intellect as dehumanized and dehumanizing.

The intellect is an enemy of the moral life only if it is confined to finding the best ways of doing things and is not also used to find what things are most worth doing. We turn to reason for assessment of means and recoil from it in choosing our ends. Wherever in the country of the mind we establish frontiers, build walls, and mount armed guards, it is the human spirit that is being imprisoned.

Kant set out to limit reason in order to make room for faith. Other philosophers instead find in the exercise of reason an expression and consummation of faith. Maimonides says of reason that it is an image of the divine in man; for Spinoza, similarly, the human mind is part of the infinite mind of God. The Hassidic master Naftali of Ropshitz remarked, "I would rather be with the wise in Hell than with the fools in Heaven—but in Heaven there are no fools!"

Kant's critique of reason was rational in the extreme; it was not rationalistic. He prefaced his work with the observation that the resistance of our institutions to such a critique "awakens a just suspicion of the soundness of their foundation." He was arguing for a reflective morality.

It is the denial that reason has any significant role in shaping the moral life which reveals a lack of faith, as though our values are too sickly to resist the germ of an idea. We need not fear for the morals of our students because of the speakers they occasionally invite to the campus; the faculty speaks to them throughout the year, with very little effect.

Rightly to be resisted is the intellectualization of the moral life, embodying the notion that values can be inculcated by sufficiently rational argument. Belief, whether about facts or values, is of slow growth; the more important the belief, the more its formation or transformation calls for sustained effort. Gray is all theory, and green the golden tree of life, says the poet. Theory is needed for cultivating trees, but theory itself will not grow them.

Obscurantism, which supposes that it is protecting values by wrapping them in mystery, evokes a counterpolar scientism, which holds that all values must either be measured or else dismissed as imponderables. Thereby, morality is diluted to a calculating prudence, and moral aspiration lowers its eyes to the bottom line. Customary morality is dressed in the borrowed finery of reflection, and values are accepted as given.

One of the founders of utilitarianism writes that when he felt that the time had come for him to marry, he chose his wife by listing all the eligible women of his acquaintance, arranging their names in order of desirability, then proposing down the list till he was accepted. He does not tell us how he decided it was time, nor how he compiled the list of eligibles and arrived at their order, nor how his future wife responded to being told that he loved her more than all but $n-1$ other women. "It is the part of an educated man," Aristotle cautioned, "to require exactness in each class of subjects only so far as the nature of the subject admits."

The question of whether virtue can be taught is as old as Plato, who sometimes speaks as if that is all that can be taught, or should be. "If you ask what is the good of education in general," he declares, "the answer is easy: that education makes good men." (Like all other men of his day, presumably he was insufficiently educated to add, "and good women.") Aristotle is characteristically straightforward: "The object of our investigation," he writes at the beginning of his treatise on ethics, "is not knowing what virtue is but to become good. . . . It is not enough to know the theory of virtue; we must endeavour to possess and apply it."

Plato held that just knowing what virtue is makes one virtuous. Philosophy is literally the love of wisdom, not merely its conceptual apprehension; one cannot grasp the Idea of the Good, Plato argued, without thereby becoming good. Something similar might be said in connection with Aristotle's "theoria" and Spinoza's "intellectual love of God."

If virtue is knowledge, it is a distinctive kind of knowing, as close to knowing *how* as to knowing *that*. Freud initially treated his patients simply by telling them what they were unconscious of. Even though they believed him, the mere telling proved to have no therapeutic effect.

The linkage between cerebral understanding and the springs of action is subtle and complex. Courses in ethics can easily bypass the linkage. When Epictetus examined the prerequisites of students who came to him to study ethics, he asked, not whether they had mastered certain subjects, but whether they had mastered their impulses. Education is food for the soul, as Socrates called it, but not if it provides only the cookbook.

In the first course in ethics I ever gave, having mentioned that Aristotle had been a tutor of Alexander the Great, I was brought up short by a student's comment, "Aristotle didn't have much luck with Alexander, did he!" My last course, in a graduate school of management, elicited from friends a similar but more blunt assessment: "You teach ethics in business and government? You're a failure!" This is the age of the expert; people suppose that morality is only another field of expertise. They confuse a healthy life with a life of health clubs.

For a time I occupied a chair in social ethics at a university in Israel. I withdrew from the chair when it became clear that the donor expected that courses in social ethics would quickly redeem a sinful generation. Higher education has no place for the appointment of an Associate Messiah, with or without tenure. What universities *can* do is to provide oases for the life of the mind—oases in which we might survive the desert winds of fanaticism, hatred, and unreason sweeping the world.

The importance to morality of the formation of good habits in childhood has been emphasized by educators as diverse as Confucius, Aristotle, Hillel, and Dewey. It is not the responsibility of the university to stand *in loco parentis*. A university is not a day-care center for late adolescence, nor a halfway house between the nursery and a place of one's own in society.

Higher education contributes less to inculcating moral values than to cultivating the tools and resources for moral reflection. The family, the church, the school, the government, and other institutions are notorious for shifting onto one another the responsibility for heightening moral sensibility and elevating moral aspiration. No doubt all of these have a part to play. For the university to recognize its limitations is not an evasion of responsibility. Higher education cannot do more, and should not be expected to do more, than all the other institutions which shape our lives.

There is a proliferation in academia of courses in ethics (usually in philosophy departments), codes of professional ethics (for instance, with regard to psychology experiments), and ethics committees (for instance, in university hospitals). All of these together, however, probably signify less than what is taught throughout the university about marketing, international relations, journalism, law, politics, and related domains of moral relevance.

Moral values (and their opposites) are taught more by example than by precept. "What you are . . . thunders so [loud] that I cannot hear what you say," Emerson explained. Providing role models for the life of the mind is itself moral education. Something else is conveyed by the anxious concern with promotion and tenure, grants and awards, publications and prizes so often evoked by academic pressures. Moral values cannot be inculcated in classes so large that students are depersonalized, even dehumanized. The pledge often printed on examination sheets, "I have neither given nor have I received help," teaches, not honesty, but self-centeredness and competitiveness.

Moral teaching is carried on by administrators, students, and alumni as well as by members of the faculty. Priorities implied by specifics of sport programs, even when these are within the limits set by athletic associations, have their effect. So also do university practices relating to investments and to accepting special conditions of bequests and endowments (for instance, by foreign governments). We do not teach equality by admissions policies which give preferential treatment to one or another racial or ethnic identity. We do not teach fraternity by saying, as did the dean of a famous law school to every entering class, "Look carefully at the two students on either side of you; next year, one of you three will not be here."

If morality imposes a duty to work for changes in society, the role of higher education is to contribute to change, not by direct action, but by the force of ideas. Education expresses the impulse to "do something about it" by action, not on the streets or in campus door-ways, but in classrooms, libraries, and laboratories. A university is a place to engage strategies of the mind, not tactics of power. It is a place for learning what to do, not for forcibly imposing decisions already arrived at elsewhere; for teach-ins, not for violent demonstra-tions. Academic freedom means that higher education is not to be a handmaiden of politics, religion, morality, or anything else, whether students, administrators, or the faculty itself seek to make it so.

Academic freedom has a counterpart: academic responsibility—to preserve and cherish the faith in the intellect. This entails unqualified respect for empirical evidence and rational argument and an unceas-ing openness to divergent opinions. It also entails a scrupulous avoid-ance of exploiting the classroom as a forum for promoting doctrines irrelevant to the presumed subject matter or of perverting any of the resources of the university to external, noneducational purposes.

Academic responsibility devolves on students as well as faculty. On entering a university, a student undertakes a commitment to be a part of a community of scholars. There is no place in a university for those who betray the commitment by interfering with speakers with whose views they disagree, disrupting teaching or research, or preventing orderly administration of the educational enterprise.

Moral obligation extends to members of the academic community as to everyone else. The dilemma of our time is that while moral responsibility remains individual, action to discharge the responsibil-ity is increasingly collective. Among the young, some eschew action— hippies and dropouts—and devote themselves to the search for moral bargains: heroism without risk, luxury without labor. Others—the activists—eschew responsibility, sacrificing personal autonomy to the demands of a movement and redefining moral norms to suit the selective morality of a political cause. Neither posture reflects moral achievement.

There is precious little moral achievement to be seen in the adult world either. Sociologists have noted that the young, especially the more educated, have ceased to believe without ceasing to be credulous. If they are more susceptible than their elders to drugs, cults, and ideologies, it is because they have not yet learned to cope with moral predicaments, nor are they yet disillusioned with promises of easy ways out of the predicaments.

Higher education responsive to moral values must make our human nature an essential part of its concerns. We do not hesitate to teach the optimal care and use of the instruments of science and technology, but not the optimal care and use of the self, the instrument of moral action. With remarkable prescience, Philo Judaeus of Alexandria asks, "Before you have made a thorough investigation of your own dwelling, is it not an excess of madness to examine that of the universe? Bring the explorer down from heaven." Moral values gain nothing by a withdrawal from any field of scientific inquiry. But inner space is as worthy of exploration as outer space. "The man who is ignorant of himself," said Spinoza, "is ignorant of the foundation of all the virtues."

Learning about oneself entails and is entailed by learning about others. This entailment has important implications for moral values. Morality is not a matter of egoism versus altruism; it is a matter of the breadth and wholeness of our identifications. As the range of identification diminishes, identity contracts to a dimensionless point. When Peer Gynt, in search of his quintessential self, peeled the layers off the wild onion, at last it crumbled in his fingers. I cannot be my brother's keeper if I do not see that I am his brother.

For me to deny my responsibility to others is to deny responsibility to myself. I am only what matters to me: my identity derives from my identifications. My identity is no more than the link between my history and my destiny; both are definable only in terms of relations to others.

"As you did it to one of the least of these my brothers," says the Gospel, "you did it to me." What happens to another happens to me if I perceive him as being mine. I do not just put myself in his place; he fills my place, which would be empty without him. The voice of my brother's blood cries out to me from the ground because it is my own blood which has been spilled. If I do not continue to demand, Let my people go! I myself remain in bondage.

Higher education can help us know who we are, whence we came, and where we are going. Providing perspectives on oneself, on society, on nature, and on the farthest reaches of the human spirit is what makes higher education higher. The cartoonist Walt Kelly, if memory serves, depicts two friends looking up at the night sky. One says to the other, "Some people believe that there are intelligent beings on planets around each of those stars. . . . Others say we are the only ones. . . . Either way, it's a sobering thought!"

Such thought is the mark of maturity. Children do not lack a sense of value, but their values are childish. As they mature, their values do not always mature with them, though the old values do not always satisfy them. Thus they do not know either what they want or what they should want, what is fulfilling and what is right. Both duty and desire are inchoate, shifting, and confused.

The business of education is to cultivate the world within, while broadening perspectives on the world without. Education is alive to moral values when it infuses knowledge with wisdom and grounds wisdom in knowledge, in ways that fix both in habit and character.

None of these things is easy to do. Fortunately, students learn much more than we teach them; they mature in both knowledge and wisdom in spite of what we do. We cannot give them what we do not have ourselves; what we do have, we cannot keep from them. The road they travel is always their own. The legend is that the Messiah is born to every generation but does not reveal himself till the generation is ready to receive him.

The question why higher education should be concerned at all with moral values answers itself. When Epictetus was challenged, "Prove to me that I should study logic!" he replied, "How will you know it is a good proof?" Where else are we to learn what life is worth living, if not in the place of learning?

One who neglects education, said Plato, walks lame to the end of his life. We teach so that no one will be crippled. When human beings walk erect, hand in hand with other human beings, they link together earth and heaven.

If I could change one thing about the university it would be to soften the impermeable barriers which separate different schools, departments, and different courses from one another. Instead of meeting rigid curricular requirements, students should be able to pursue interdisciplinary programs; instead of meeting rigid course requirements students should be able to engage in guided reading and discussions in tutorials. What is truly learned is only what is appropriate to individual capacities and interests.

Academic changes, even though they are in intellectual content and not only in administrative forms, can easily remain purely academic. Yet the changes I envision may make for greater perspective and—we need not abandon the term—relevance. Immoral conduct is often, perhaps always, illiberal in its preconceptions—narrow, remote, and dogmatic. Liberal education cannot guarantee moral achievement, but it might very well preserve us from the moral degradations of fanaticism.

THE ROLE OF A WESTERN UNIVERSITY IN FORMING A SOCIAL MORALITY

2

James H. Billington

THERE ARE TWO SUBJECTS here that one is trying to connect: morality in our society and the nature of a university. Neither subject is much discussed in our public culture. But both the fabric of our society and the functioning of our universities may well be in deep trouble. It is disturbing that neither our political nor our educational leaders seem to be aware that there is much of a problem.

It may be, as Mr. Kaplan suggests, that our generation is no more sinful than any other—perhaps in some respects less so. Per capita consumption of alcohol was three times higher in America in 1830 than it is now. But there is a special quality to the moral callousness of our times. We have quite simply created a public culture in which selfishness has itself become almost the major social virtue. The calf of gold has grown into a bull. It is worshipped in a culture that glorifies personal economic aggrandizement, by promoting consumer self-indulgence with civic self-indulgence (emphasizing group entitlements over civic duties) as the only remedy. One system has produced a coddled "me generation" of students. A recent study based on a poll of the graduating class at one of our leading universities

James H. Billington is Librarian of Congress, Washington, D.C.

quoted this seemingly successful and success-bound body as collectively concluding:

> If you can't be sure of anything, then get a good job and try to put some distance between yourself and the coming hard times.

In other words, having finished the rat race, keep on running—and preferably away from the others, because the ship may be going down and it's every rat for himself. Maybe we are all fellow passengers not on Spaceship Earth (the standard metaphor for moralists these days), but rather on some new version of the *Titanic*—a vessel crowded with those who indulge themselves but no longer reach out to others. There may be a cold retribution lying ahead. Nordic legend imagined Hell as eternal ice, not perpetual flame. We may get there not via the intelligentsia's old apocalyptical scenario of a cold war leading to nuclear winter. The end may come not with a big bang, but with a thousand whimpers, as we turn in on ourselves and imperceptibly descend from medium cool into a culture of perhaps irretrievable human coldness.

There are, of course, tremendous countervailing forces of vitality and altruism in our society—in the voluntary private sector of church and community groups (of which Tocqueville spoke so admiringly) and in many public service professions, and even within the government. What is striking, however, is that these forces receive so little attention—let alone encouragement—from the major forces that largely define our public culture and shared values: political leaders, dispensers of private wealth, the national media, and the elite universities.

I would not pretend to have made a systematic study of any of these four powerful groups; but I see alarming signs in all four. So, without pretending that things were better in the old days, let us see what the problems are in our own days—the only ones we will ever know and be responsible for.

GOVERNMENT LEADERS

Although moral questions are much talked about by politicians, there seems to me to have been remarkably little personal attention paid by political leaders in recent decades to the sources of local initiative and altruism that do exist and could be encouraged in our society: what some have called the "mediating structures" between the state and the individual. In terms of concrete commitment, the account seems rather meager—for either personal contributions of time and money, or institutional leadership in convening major conferences or serious legislation.

The two traditional bulwarks of moral formation in our society—religious institutions and the family—can never be created by (and should not be identified with) the state; but they could well be given more scope to perform their part of the public agenda than they have been allowed to do in recent years. Our public culture seems to have gone beyond the liberal virtue of showing more tolerance and understanding for diversity in social arrangements and sexual practices to insisting that the public culture attribute equal value to all norms. President Carter, a man of incontestable personal commitment to the monogamous family, found himself in his public capacity sanctioning this relativism about norms when he acquiesced in renaming his proposed White House gathering on the family a conference on "families." President Reagan, who was eloquent in attempting to get government bureaucracy out of the human needs agenda, did not seem to have made a comparable effort to get the private sector more deeply into it. President Bush attaches great importance to these "thousand points of light" in the voluntary sector, but he does not initially at least seem to have found the response or support needed to upgrade their importance.

DISPENSERS OF PRIVATE WEALTH

The moral callousness of the newly rich seems particularly striking. One of our most deeply philanthropic corporate chief executives recently spoke with sadness about the seeming indifference to any form of philanthropy by whole categories of the young, new millionaires, whom he described (more in sorrow than in anger) as the most profoundly selfish people he had ever met.

While the little people of this country seem to be giving as much or more than ever to the family, church, and other local human services, the impression grows that many big people are increasingly indifferent. It may not be accidental that so much of this new wealth is gained from the unreal paper world of leveraged buy outs, stock speculation, and litigation, rather than from the production of commodities of direct use to people. We have become a society that consumes far more than it produces—living off our capital perhaps spiritually as well as economically.

THE NATIONAL MEDIA

The influence of the national media—television above all—on the formation of shared values is as all-permeating as it is difficult to characterize precisely. A study a few years ago (that is no doubt already outmoded) estimated that television runs on for seven and a half hours a day in 98 percent of American homes, exposing the average American, by the time he is eighteen years old, to more than 13,000 killings, 100,000 violent episodes, and half a million commercials. Even soap operas, situation comedies, talk shows, and quiz shows increasingly decouple sex from marriage and lend a lustrous sparkle to it all. Television is inherently corrosive of religious faith (despite—perhaps because of—the electronic churches). A recent survey of 140 randomly selected leaders in television showed that while 93 percent had a religious upbringing, 93 percent seldom or never attended religious services. Television tends to undermine not just religion, but civic commitment and involvement of all sorts. It encourages a passive spectatorism that destroys interest in issues and participation in their resolution—and thus the maintenance of elementary civil decencies and some measure of common purpose among a pluralistic people.

The root problem in our society is the decoupling of freedom from responsibility. This problem has its political dimension. Conservatives seek freedom from the government without accepting personal responsibility for the things government has been asked to do. Liberals seek freedom from personal responsibility by transferring as many problems as possible to impersonal bureaucracies. The problem within our leadership groups is not simply that they are by and large in flight from their forefathers' sense of personal accountability to the Judeo-

Christian God of Judgment; we have also tended to reject the related historic belief in an objective moral order to the universe. Our elite culture increasingly seems to believe in a subjective aesthetic disorder that is self-created. There is an increasing fascination with the aesthetics of power rather than the content of policy—and a tendency to indulge (out of spiritual boredom more than reformist conviction) synthetic and transient trends in politics and art no less than fashion. This confusion of the moral and aesthetic inclines us to look in the wrong place for both goodness and beauty.

True goodness is found among people and is fulfilled in human association; true beauty is found in things and fulfilled in material nature. But our culture has twisted it all around and taught us to worship the false gods of "beautiful people" and the so-called "good things of life." In the city where I live, people often turn first in the morning to a part of the newspaper called "style," which keeps everyone posted on the movements of all those beautiful people. Admiring physical beauty more than true goodness in people is characteristic of the unrecognized neopaganism of our times. Many of our celebrated national afflictions—narcissism, indulgence in pornography, and sheer loneliness—are related to our excessive worship of beauty as the object, the body as the subject, the mirror as our icon. Life itself in our public culture sometimes seems more a matter of style than substance. Hence the arrival of that dreadful word "life-style."

If life is just a matter of style, one is just as good as another; and one after another is no doubt best of all.

But no one can live that way; and no society will long endure or even cohere without some basic moral standards. Sooner or later, if they are not found within, they will be imposed from without.

THE ELITE UNIVERSITIES

So what is the role of the university—the last of our four leadership groups—in causing or in curing this national malady? I believe that educational institutions in general (and universities in particular) are probably the *least* responsible of the leadership groups here discussed for the erosion of morals in our country. Our higher educational system is properly designed in a pluralistic society to be an inculcator of intellectual standards and critical faculties rather than of moral norms. Nevertheless, the universities do have an important role to play that they have been reluctant to acknowledge, let alone exercise.

Perhaps the most serious dereliction of higher educational institutions under the pressures of the 1960s was their simple failure to uphold intellectual standards—a failure now widely acknowledged and (at least in some areas) being corrected. But our unprecedented national investment in higher education has been made over the centuries in the belief that colleges and universities were producing moral citizens for a free and open society—not just reproducing scholars for closed academic guilds. If we are to continue to send such large numbers of late adolescents on to four more years of full-time education after secondary school, the institutions concerned will have to make some contribution to reuniting freedom with responsibility. The fact is, however, that, far from helping inculcate responsibility, the universities have become in many ways privileged preserves indulging individual freedom without any responsibility at all. The tenured faculty has few enforceable responsibilities to students who in turn seek all the privileges of adults with none of the responsibilities. Administrations spend their time adjusting to the students' right to do this or that rather than defining, let alone enforcing, responsibilities.

Although the old rules were often difficult to enforce and sometimes downright repressive, the new situation in which no one publicly defines a norm creates campuses full of lonely people held together more by occasional animal ritual than by any sense of richer human community. The only shared moral enthusiasms are often about symbolic issues and distant causes. Universities tend to encourage intense moralism about such matters even as they indulge near total permissiveness on immediate personal questions.

One reason that there is a periodic flight in the modern university to moral absolutism about some passing and contingent political cause is the spiritual starvation of living in an allegedly value-free curriculum. The brighter students realize that universities in fact impart values under the guise of imparting none. The values are often simply those either of the consumer society or of the modern academic substitutes for religion: ideologies and methodologies.

In my own discipline of history, to take one example, the prevailing mode of thought suggests that people's actions are guided not so much by moral choice as by socioeconomic pressures and psychosexual drives. This conveys a sense that history is made by impersonal forces—diminishing the importance of individual choice and of the moral component in that choice. The emphasis on determinism tends to minimize the importance of what is most human about people—their anguish, achievements, and aspirations. This view of people helps make us a less caring society—and may also play a role in the decreasing enthusiasm for public life and public service.

Let me say clearly what may so far have been only implied: Universities do not bear the major share of the blame, and they are too fragile to bear a major share of the remedies needed to check the erosion of shared values in our free society. In a democracy with a plurality of institutions and interests, it is too much to ask one institution already overloaded with expectations to provide answers in the moral—let alone the spiritual—sphere, when its special function is primarily to train the critical intellect.

Yet, it seems to me, universities *can* properly be asked to devote more of their energies to rectifying—in ways appropriate to their own special nature—three basic failings that they have permitted to become embedded in their own structures. These three failings keep the modern megaversity from playing the role it properly should in giving better moral shape to the broader society. If it would be dangerous to ask too much of the university, it would be demeaning to ask too little of it.

First, universities have generally given up on the task of imparting to their students basic knowledge about their own Western tradition. The essentials of the classical and Judeo-Christian heritage and the basic facts about the European and American history that has shaped us—none of this is deemed essential anymore.

The university may be the only place where the outmoded industrial assembly line is still the basic form of organization. The modern research university remains an efficient production stream for forcing its younger faculty into narrow specialization and the production of new monographs. Some quality can surely be winnowed out of all the quantity of scholarly writing. But even by the standards of the market, this procedure is profoundly inadequate. It degrades scholarship by flooding the market with second-rate works clothed in jargon and pretense, and it produces a classic crisis of economic overproduction: more and more books for less and less readers—thereby lowering rather than raising the rate of civilized literacy needed for a healthy democracy.

While one can produce a whole car through assembly-line specialization, one can never produce a whole person that way. And without whole people with strong civic involvement and deep personal convictions, democracy cannot function—as George Washington eloquently warned in the now rather neglected parts of his Farewell Address.

If the universities as a whole are still held back by the outmoded industrial model of an overspecialized scholarly assembly line, the humanistic core of the curriculum seems equally held back by its mimicry of another anachronistic model—the positivistic methods of late nineteenth-century natural science. The research structure of the humanities and social sciences is totally attuned to (and likely to reward) those who come up with smart new ways of cutting things up. No one is putting things back together; and the student is left with a consumer-oriented, smorgasbord curriculum that bends over backwards to avoid seeming even to suggest that Shakespeare might be more worth reading than Beckett, the Bible more than Nietzsche.

If we are going to hold together as a people and continue to devote so much time to higher education—both in my view desirable goals—we have to put at least a few things back together. We need, in short, a common core of shared readings (if not courses) that all students must take—in which the great classics are read and discussed. Each institution can draw up its own core. The very act of deciding what to include could be a unifying act within an institution—and would make the transmission of that part of the human heritage that deals with values a conscious and dignified part of faculty commitment.

Nothing could be more specious than the argument that an emphasis on our own Western values will cut us off from other people in our new global era. Others do not respect those lacking in self-respect. A deeper understanding of one's own culture is a reenforcement (if not a prerequisite) for understanding another's culture. Far from providing a curriculum that enables us to understand non-Western cultures better, the morally amnesiac modern university has produced a curriculum emancipated from any sense of tradition at all.

Second, universities have generally given up any sense of responsibility for providing their students with positive role models. Moral education is more effectively caught than taught; and there is always a thirst among adolescents for people they can look up to about how to live as well as how to think. College students are learning about both at the same time in a kind of tribal community. The question is not *whether* the university is teaching both subjects, but *what* is being taught and *how*. The thirst for affirmative example is even greater today with so many coming from broken family backgrounds to large and impersonal campus communities. The moral education that students seek is likely to degenerate into counterproductive didacticism or even downright demagogic anti-intellectualism in such an atmosphere unless it is embodied in the context of lives rather than the content of lectures.

Universities need, quite simply, role models among their faculty, administrators, and coaches. There seems to me an inescapable need to tackle the difficult problem of making more of an effort particularly in recruiting graduate students but also in hiring faculty to bring in people committed to personal values as well as to intellectual discipline. One would worry if moral commitment were required; but in many academic disciplines today the problem is just the opposite: such commitments are discouraged and may even be a disqualification.

Part of the problem may be the pretence that everyone teaching in a university is also a scholar working on the frontiers of knowledge. It might be desirable to bring into the humanities courses of a university a new category of teachers who are not formally academic scholars, but rather people of high intelligence and wide experience anxious to take up a second career of teaching in the humanities at a more advanced age. We turn out to pasture too much high talent at an early age in this society; and an infusion of mature and experienced people into the teaching of the great classics could bring a breath of fresh air from real-life experience into the academic hothouse where inexperienced adolescents are taught by people who have learned about human problems only from books and charts. If carefully chosen – as were the original preceptors brought in by Woodrow Wilson to enliven Princeton at the beginning of this century – a new body of people chosen to teach and, in effect, be leaders for students could also stimulate faculties. Such people – because they would already have pursued careers in the broader world – could take away some of the burden of role modelling from academic scholars, who, if properly chosen, will never provide more than a modest share of the broader models for the society as a whole.

The third failure of the modern university poses the most difficult question of all: Is there a role in the modern American university for the direct transmission of values and beliefs by people who believe in them? Historically, our private university system at least arose out of the desire to transmit religious beliefs along with education. The modern university has not just quietly removed that function; it has in fact created a dominant new subculture of alienation from both traditional religious and common patriotic values. Bringing into university communities people with some experience of actively serving their country (a species increasingly absent from most campuses) would help fill the latter lacuna; but the lack of patriotic voices on campus does not seem to me the major part of the problem. The modern national state has plenty of ways of inculcating loyalties and conformities and there could be real risks in intruding nationalist ideology into campus curricula. The proper way to inculcate a mature sense of patriotism seems to me the institution of a national service requirement for the young that would not be confined solely to military options but would be fulfilled before going to college.

It seems to me at least worth discussing two possibilities that are rarely even considered in polite society.

One possibility would be the reexamination by institutions that have distinctive denominational traditions of ways that those traditions can be used to affirm norms either through the curriculum or through other aspects of the shared life on their particular campus. Far from representing a return to bigotry or the exclusion of others, such institutional reexaminations represent the greatest possible service to those of other faiths and persuasions. Precisely by finding everything of value and deeper relevance in one's own tradition, one helps others find similar reserves of strength in their own. Pluralism implies a variety of deeply held convictions, not a monism of indifference in which all convictions are deemed equally irrelevant. One of the saddest features of contemporary higher education is its compulsive imitativeness. We need to break not just with the assembly-line faculty, but also with the idea that the best professors are interchangeable parts in a scholarly market with no local attachments or personal convictions. We need different schools teaching different things. Many more institutions should find the courage to follow their own paths; and all of us will benefit.

Within the larger, public institutions that may not have a common tradition to reaffirm in new ways, there may be another way of satisfying the thirst for some education in values among the young. It might be possible to follow the example of released time for religious instruction in public secondary schools by granting a kind of course credit for, say, two or three courses that represent the core teaching of one great religion or other value system. These courses should perhaps include one course on the core teachings and a second course that applies those teachings to contemporary personal and social problems. After all, if one can require someone to swim fifty yards before graduation, one might be justified in requiring everyone to swim through at least one of the great religions or moral systems of mankind.

Human Awareness and Moral Values in Higher Education

3

Ivana Marková

THE QUESTION OF MORAL VALUES in higher education is part of a broader issue of the function of the university as such. The university as an institution is part of the life of the community, and the degree to which it promotes moral values and moral norms closely reflects the promotion of values and norms in the community as a whole. So we must ask ourselves whether the university plays any special role in the promotion of moral values and, if it does, what are the characteristics of this role that differentiate the university from the rest of the community and from other institutions. In order to answer this question I shall focus on the phenomenon of reflexive awareness with respect to moral values.

According to Hegel human beings are characterized by two fundamental features.[1] First, they have the capacity to acknowledge others as human beings. Secondly, they can not only acknowledge humanity in others but also have the need to be acknowledged as such by them. These two features can be traced to the origin of mankind and one can find them in various human societies. They are also expressed in the Christian "love your neighbor as yourself" (Matthew 22:39, New

Ivana Marková is a professor of psychology at the University of Stirling, Scotland.

English Bible). One can say that the human spirit really exists only to the extent to which people confirm each other in this way.[2]

The degree to which people acknowledge each other, and the level of awareness with which they do so, have undergone essential changes in the history of mankind with respect to social, cultural, political, economic, and religious factors. It has been argued by many that the present level of self- and other-awareness in Western culture reflects the growth of individualism in the last two or three hundred years.[3] Historians of human self-consciousness have maintained that subjective self-awareness as we know it today has appeared relatively recently in human history. It did not exist in ancient cultures such as the Myceanaean, about three thousand years ago. Jaynes argued that the people of the Myceanaean culture had no words to express their subjective mental states and that therefore they had no awareness of such states.[4] But even if one disagrees with such a theory, the existence of slavery, racism, and other sinister forms of discrimination among people points to the fact that the acknowledgment of humanity applied—and still applies—to some people but not to others. To dismiss another person's comment in a conversation, to deliberately ignore the other's question, to be uncaring about the thoughts and feelings of the other person—all of them in little ways exemplify the fact that confirmation of the other's humanity in its entirety is difficult to maintain at various levels of interaction and relationship. Indeed, we rarely give full justice to this fundamental feature of humanity.

I argue in this essay that, in our present Western culture, acknowledgment of humanity means acknowledgment of *reflexive agency* and therefore of *moral agency*. A morality based on reflexive agency is highly demanding because it requires perpetual monitoring of action and reflexion in the world of constant change in which we live. It is my conviction that our present society, both at the community and at the university levels, has failed to cope with our reflexive agency in the social world that we have created and that, consequently, we appear to be in a state of imminent moral collapse. I focus in this essay on one aspect only of our inability to cope with our reflexive agency—namely, on the relationship between knowledge and morality. In particular, I argue that while people, in general, have developed reflexive self-awareness, they still largely operate with a pre-reflexive conception of knowledge that separates itself from morality.

I

In his study of the history of the family in England from the sixteenth to the nineteenth century, Stone provides an excellent analysis of the forces leading to the rise of individualism and of modern self- and other-awareness.[5] In addition to economic pressure and the growth and mobility of the population, among the forces of particular interest are Calvinist theology and morality, and the growth of public literacy. Both of these reinforced soul-searching and introspection, though in different ways. The printing revolution, too, encouraging the growth of literacy, had important effects on societal and psychological change. While sociologists of knowledge and historians have usually focused their attention on political and economic change in the transition from medieval to modern European society, Eisenstein has demonstrated that printing and literacy were equally important agents of change.[6] In addition to public self-learning and the promotion of motivation for individual achievement, literacy contributed to the increasing level of reflexivity. While in 1841, in England, about half of the women and one-third of the men were still illiterate, with the introduction of compulsory school education reading became more widespread. A written text, it has been argued, more than spoken words, makes it possible for the reader to look back and to interpret and reinterpret the text.[7] There is also considerable psychological evidence that literacy is related to reflexivity[8] and that as the child grows older, his or her reflexive ability increases.[9]

Mead argued convincingly that reflexive self-awareness as the common human phenomenon that we know today is the product of the romanticism of the nineteenth century.[10] I prefer to talk, in this same context, of expressivism to characterize the broadly based spiritual movement that reacted strongly against the prevailing rationalism of the time.[11] This movement, of course, included romanticism. There were two particular aspects of expressivism that contributed greatly to the growth of reflexive self-awareness. The first was the ability to become an object of one's observation, and the second was the emphasis on practical activity.

The expressivists' realization of the existence of different cultures, values, and moral standards led to the idea of putting oneself in the shoes of others and attempting to see the world through their eyes. This ability to look at the world through the eyes of others also enables one to look at oneself through the eyes of others: the self becomes reflexively self-aware; that is, it becomes an object of its own observation. Hand in hand with the emphasis on practical activity that was so important for the economic growth of the eighteenth and nineteenth centuries, the idea that people become aware of themselves through their active experience of, and interference with, the world was supported by expressivism. Hegel maintained that it is through their own action upon the world—that is, through practical involvement—that people not only transform things but also change themselves and gain self-knowledge.[12] The idea that human beings are on an odyssey—that is, are pilgrims who, on their journey in the world and through their own active transformation of the world, eventually come to recognize themselves—was quite common in nineteenth-century German literature, philosophy, and social science. It was also a fundamental idea in Goethe's *Faust*. The essence of this motif can be conceived as based on a three-step development. First, pilgrims who return from their journey through the world are different from what they were at the beginning of the journey because of their activities during that journey. Second, the world itself is different because of the pilgrims' activities affecting it. Third, the world appears to be different to the pilgrims after completion of their journey not only because their activities have had an effect on the world but because their activities have also had a profound effect on themselves: their experience and perception both of the world and of themselves is now different.

Thus, it was in expressivism that one learned to look at oneself as an *object*, which resulted from one's ability to take the role or the attitude of others toward oneself. Moreover, one also became aware of oneself as a *subject*, as a doer who can influence changes in the world. These two aspects of self-awareness, that is, the *self as object* and the *self as subject* seem to have appeared first in the work of Kant and

Hegel. In psychology, it was James[13] and then Mead[14] to whom we owe the distinction between the *I*, the self as an *agent*, as a *subject*, and the *Me*, the self as a *reflexive being*, as an *object*. Reflexivity as a phenomenon, of course, existed a long time ago and one is fully aware of it in Plato's dialogues just as in Shakespeare's dramas. It is, however, reflexivity as a societal phenomenon that emerged with the growth of literacy that is a focus of this essay. Its penetration of societal institutions is of particular interest in our discussion of moral values in higher education.

II

The university established itself in the Middle Ages primarily as an institution cultivating the intellect. Over the centuries the assumptions as to why and how the intellect should be cultivated have undergone changes, both in overall strategy and in detail, focusing at one time on the promotion of knowledge and at another on the education of good citizens. The nineteenth century was a time of university expansion both in Europe and the United States, and the question of the function of the university came to the fore. This was a time of rapid development in science and technology and many educationalists were preoccupied with the form that a modern university should take. With the sciences increasingly introduced into university curricula, questions of the role of research and professional training were added to those emphasizing the cultivation of the intellect and the importance of knowledge. For example, Flexner, in his historical treatise of American, British, and German universities, maintained that the university had four major concerns. These included the conservation and interpretation of knowledge and ideas, the search for truth, and the training of students.[15] Ashby, in his historical analysis of the function of the university, also focused his attention on the conservation, advancement, and transmission of knowledge.[16] On the other hand, in his *Mission of the University*, José Ortega y Gasset forcibly argued that it is the transmission of culture, together with the teaching of the professions and scientific research, that are the major functions of the university.[17]

In the history of Western culture, concern with the conservation, transmission, and advancement of knowledge has traditionally been associated with the search for certainty, truth, and objectivity, which were assumed to be neutral with respect to individual human beings. From ancient philosophy to the modern philosophy of the seventeenth and eighteenth centuries the search for universally valid laws — for true, immutable, and eternal essences — was ubiquitous. Impartiality and neutrality were essential presuppositions of any search for truth. This conception is thus based on the assumption that *knowledge* exists quite apart from individual human beings — that is, apart from the *knowers*. All the knowers can do is to aim at the discovery of natural laws, eternal universals, and the truth. This conception, which separates knowledge from the knower and treats the two as independent entities, corresponds, historically and culturally, to a pre-reflexive level of human awareness. It is a distinct feature of epistemology from Plato to Descartes and Kant. It idealizes immutable universals and is contemptuous of particulars — that is, of things that emerge, exist for a while, and then disintegrate.

Just as in this pre-reflexive, pre-Hegelian conception of human awareness, knowledge is separated from the knower, so, too, morality as a universal is separated from the individual moral agent. This claim can be clarified as follows. According to Kantian morality, a person is a rational agent. Being a rational agent, a person recognizes, by definition, *the good* and ought to act in accordance with the universal moral law of the categorical imperative. Morality in this conception is a sense of duty, immutable, impartial, and neutral with respect to the individual. Kant expressed this view of moral consciousness in his saying that people should act always as if the maxim of their action was to become a universal law.[18] Hegel was critical of such a concept of universal morality, in which the individual's subjective identity and particular personal circumstances had no role to play whatsoever. In his essay *The Spirit of Christianity and Its Fate*, analyzing Kant's conception of morality, Hegel contrasted the moral criteria involved in the Old and New Testaments.[19]

Just as with Kantian morality, so, according to Hegel, with the morality of the Old Testament: both were based on immutable moral universals. The morality of the Old Testament was guided by the Ten

Commandments that had to be accepted by people without question, passively, and as a duty to their Lawgiver. As Hegel puts it, "A passive people giving laws to itself would be a contradiction."[20] In contrast, it was Jesus, in the New Testament, who introduced a new kind of morality, which was based on the right of the individual to make personal judgments. Thus he brought subjectivity and individual moral action into morality. While morality in the Old Testament was abstract and based on the *form* of the law and on what people ought to do, morality in the New Testament was based on the *content* of the law that enabled people to judge its applicability for themselves. While the former was based on the command to obey, the latter was based on the ability of people to love others.

This change in the focus of morality was not just a change from obeying to loving, but, more importantly, a change in the focus of human awareness itself. While the former requires unquestioning submission to a powerful God, the latter, as Hegel says elsewhere, means that "true union, or love proper, exists, only between living beings who are alike in power and thus in one another's eyes living beings from every point of view."[21] One can extend this claim by saying that only living beings equal in power could confirm each other as such. Although people may love animals, they do not expect to gain the kind of respect from them that they can, at least in principle, gain from fellow human beings. Hegel thus confronted moral objectivity and neutrality with morality based on human subjectivity. In this view, the individual "has barriers only where he erects them himself, and his virtues are determinacies which he fixes himself."[22] At the same time, however, a morality based on love is not a subjectivistic kind of morality claiming that the individual is the only criterion of moral standards. Morality based on love reaches toward the other person, and at its most general level to mankind as such. Having contrasted the two kinds of morality in the context of the Judeo-Christian tradition, Hegel delivered a clear message: moral action directed to the other individual treats the other with the same respect as that with which one treats oneself.

If morality means moral action based on respect for the other person, the relationship between morality and knowledge can now be clarified. It has been pointed out already that the pre-Hegelian conceptions of knowledge and morality assumed both universality and immutability. In the case of knowledge, this position was not challenged by pre-Hegelian philosophy. The natural sciences, which were only in their infancy at that time, did not have much effect on the life of the individual and, indeed, it was not expected that they would have any practical use. Thus, in the eighteenth century there were numerous public demonstrations of scientific discoveries—for example, of static electricity. A pretty lady assistant would be suspended on silk cords, her feet rubbing against a rotating glass globe, and a man in the audience enticed up to the platform to kiss her, whereupon he received a somewhat unpleasant electric shock. Such demonstrations were for public amusement. The nineteenth century, however, rapidly changed the situation and a utilitarian point of view became the slogan of the day. It was in the spirit of the desire to know what things are for that Michael Faraday was challenged by a woman at a demonstration of electromagnetism at one of the Royal Institution's famous Friday Evening Discourses. "But Mr. Faraday, of what *use* is it?" Faraday, it is said, replied: "Madam, of what use is a baby?" Advances in science and technology demonstrated very clearly the potential practical consequences of the discoveries in pure physics, chemistry, and biology; of the cure of disease; of enhancements in the speed of communication; and of industrial innovations—and thus the consequences for the lives of individuals. Knowledge, suddenly, was directly relevant to individuals, and it became important how it was used. Science and technology were now seen as having moral implications, and the traditional conception of neutral and objective science was thrown into confusion.

Philosophically, there was Hegel's solution to this problem. However, it was in general ignored as irrelevant to science. In Kant's conceptual framework, the laws of nature and moral laws were conceived as totally different in kind and mutually independent of each other. Nature was governed by totally different rules than moral consciousness, and moral consciousness was indifferent to nature. Hegel argued strongly against this split between nature and moral action. His argument is complex and we shall consider it in two steps: first with respect to knowledge, and second with respect to moral action. The first part of the argument, in a simplified form, is as follows.

Traditional Cartesian epistemology postulated, on the one hand, the existence of the world as it is, and, on the other hand, that of the cognizing subject. The problem that this division created was how the cognizing subject could know that what is cognized is true, that is, that the world cognized is the world in itself. Traditional epistemology could give no satisfactory answer to this question, since there could be no independent access to the world itself by which one's cognition of it could be judged. For Hegel the whole problem is incoherent because what the knowing subject has access to is not the world as it is but the world as it is for the knower. Knowing the world is a process in which the knower and the object of his or her knowledge both undergo transformation. The object is the standard against which knowledge is measured; it is the testing criterion of knowledge. Since the object can only be the object that is perceived or cognized, the object that is the standard lies within the knower rather than in the outside world. Further, because one's knowledge of an object in part determines one's cognition of the object, the standard against which knowledge is measured itself changes as knowledge of it progresses. If the knower's concept of the object satisfies the testing criterion, there are no grounds for a change in either the knower of the object or in the object of his or her knowledge.

Such satisfaction, however, is usually only temporary. Once knowers increase their involvement they find that what appeared to be coherent on the surface suffers from internal contradictions, and therefore a solution of such contradictions is required. By being able to solve the contradictions between their temporary concepts and temporary testing criteria, the knowers understand not only the objects of their knowledge but also themselves. In addition, they are now more free because they can better control the objects, knowing them better, and they can also make more meaningful decisions about the objects, and also better control their own course of action. Thus, in Hegel's conception, knowledge in general is gained through self-knowledge, because as knowledge in general becomes more adequate, so self-knowledge also becomes more adequate. Gaining self-knowledge, however, is a social phenomenon, as already pointed out. One gains self-knowledge by being able to look at oneself and one's own activities through the eyes of others. It is this claim, therefore, that brings together acquisition of knowledge and moral or reflexive agency. Since knowers are reflexive beings, knowledge as moral action has moral implications for them as *individuals,* as members of particular *social groups,* and for *mankind* as a whole. If one accepts that people have a capacity for moral awareness, that is, an awareness of themselves in terms of others and of others in terms of themselves, then the separation between knowledge and morality disappears. Rather, it is through acting upon nature that we become aware of ourselves as reflexive agents and practice our moral self-consciousness. Knowledge gives us responsibility for ourselves and for others since we can both act and reflect on our action. To be self-conscious and reflexive, in a modern sense, means to be aware of oneself in terms of others and of others in terms of oneself. It is in this sense that to know is to act morally.

III

The question of the place of moral values in the university appears to be relatively new. Cardinal Newman, in his discourses on the nature of university education, made it quite clear that the university was a place for the teaching of universal knowledge and that its object was "intellectual, not moral."[23] As far as I am aware, in the United Kingdom the issue of moral values at universities only assumed importance after the Second World War. Moberly explicitly refers to the moral collapse of the German universities under the pressure of the Nazi regime. Educationally and intellectually, German universities enjoyed recognition as having achieved the highest standards of the nineteenth century; and their examples were followed by other countries, including the United Kingdom and the United States, in their conception of a modern university. However, with their universal approach to morality they were destitute, so that they could offer little or no resistance to the monstrous Nazi ideology. Moberly argued that the German universities, in spite of having high intellectual standards, had no independent standards or values that would guard them against evil doctrines.[24] Such an academic neutrality, indolent and unprepared for challenge, seems to me to be part and parcel of the idea that knowledge and morality are two different, totally independent issues, and that the role of universities is to be concerned with the former but not with the latter issue. In the United States similar views have been recently voiced by many scholars.[25] Consider several examples illustrating this problem.

A friend of mine, Dr. Alice Heim of Cambridge University, once told me the story of a very bright young man, competent in many school subjects, who had difficulty in deciding which career to choose. He was therefore sent for testing of his aptitudes, personality characteristics, and intelligence. He scored very highly on intelligence and all kinds of aptitudes but very low on interest in other people and ability to relate to other people. On the basis of the test he was recommended to study—experimental psychology. In fact, the psychology taught at many universities is such that it was not such a ludicrous recommendation for a young man after all. Students learn about perception, cognitive processes, artificial intelligence, animal learning, psychometric testing—but hardly at all about people. The methods of psychology are claimed to be objective. Questionnaires, interview schedules, and tests must be scientifically validated for the purpose of research. Preferably, the experimental psychologist speaks to his or her subjects (words such as "people," "participants," or "patients" are not sufficiently scientific) as little as possible in order not to bias their reactions in one way or another. Such pseudo-objective methods dehumanize both the experimenter and his or her subject. The subject is dehumanized because he or she is not considered, at least for the purpose of the experiment, to be a reflexive agent. The person is assumed to react to the stimuli presented with no consideration of his or her reflexivity. The experimenter dehumanizes himself or herself by treating the other as a physical object devoid of reflexive agency.

Another example concerns the selection of students, in the United Kingdom, for the study of medicine. Competition for a place at a medical school is very severe, and successful candidates are expected to have very high grades in physics and mathematics. The general assumption on which the entry criteria for medicine are based is that physics and mathematics, rather than other school subjects, are particularly sensitive indicators of the intellectual capacity of a person and therefore the most sensitive indicators of the likelihood of becoming a good doctor. It is taken for granted that to be a good doctor means to be a good scientist rather than to have compassion for one's fellow human beings. None of us, of course, would want doctors to have compassion but be inadequately equipped in medicine, which would be the other extreme of the existing system. The issue I have raised, of course, is not new. More than forty years ago, Ortega y Gasset discussed the same issue in his *Mission of the University.*

> The medical schools aspire to teach physiology and chemistry complete to the nth degree; but perhaps in no medical school the world over is there anyone seriously occupied with thinking out what it really means to be a good physician, what the ideal type should be for our times. The profession, which after culture is the most urgent concern, is entrusted largely to the kindness of Providence. But the harm of our confused procedure has worked both ways. Science too has suffered by our wishful attempt to bring it into line alongside the professions.[26]

Ortega rejected overspecialization in university teaching, claiming that "barbarians of specialization" educated in their very narrow fields did nothing to transmit culture. By "culture" he meant the vital system of ideas of the period concerning the world and humanity. For him, the teaching of culture was the basic function of the university, with the teaching of the professions and research following close behind. If people did not learn the culture into which they were born, they were unable to communicate with, or indeed take a reflexive attitude to, anybody outside their profession. Ortega referred, in this context, to the wisdom of a Chinese thinker, Chuang-tsu, who lived in the fourth century B.C. In Chuang-tsu's book, the God of the Northern Sea was concerned with the problem of communicating with those who have not experienced the culture of others and therefore were incapable of taking their point of view:

> How shall I talk of the sea to the frog, if he has never left this pond? How shall I talk of the frost to the bird of the summer land, if it has never left the land of its birth? How shall I talk of life with the sage, if he is the prisoner of his doctrine?[27]

Moberly also refers disparagingly to the looker-on approach of many academic scholars, with their false neutrality and inability to make a decision because of the fear that they might get it wrong.[28]

The attitude that one must learn how to live before actually living, to accumulate data for something one never uses, still prevails among many. Thought divorced from responsible action, Moberly argues, is sterile, and a purely theoretical analysis is liable to lead to impotence.[29] It was this false passivity and neutrality that rendered German students and scholars unable to resist Nazism. Although the function of universities is to promote intellectual understanding, such a function cannot be fulfilled if academic thought is sterile and thus morally defective.

This attitude of false neutrality and pseudo-objectivity prevails not only in higher education but also in primary and secondary schools. One of the present controversial issues is sex education in schools. It is increasingly believed that pre-teenage children should be taught the "facts of life." In their classes on sex education, children are informed about the biological facts of reproduction and sexual intercourse, of contraceptive methods, of alternative methods of making love in order to prevent pregnancy, and so on. Girls under the age of sixteen can obtain contraceptives from a general practitioner without the knowledge of their parents. Education and policies of this kind are carried out in the spirit of the right to be fully informed and the right to decide for oneself issues that concern oneself. This attitude, however, is based on the implicit assumption that there is such a thing as objective information and knowledge, and that this objective information and knowledge exists on its own quite independently of any individual human being. In other words, twentieth-century education operates, in this as in other cases, with a pre-reflexive conception of knowledge. Yet it is a well-documented fact that giving people this kind of objective knowledge is ineffectual for them as individuals. It may be harmful. For example, cases of cervical cancer due to early sexual intercourse have increased by ten times or so in the last decade. In spite of the tremendous amount of money spent on health education, giving people information, and only information, about the hazards of smoking and drugs does not work. To put it in a different way, telling people how to act on a piece of information without teaching them how to relate the information to themselves as human beings, in my view, fails to achieve its objective because it lacks reflexivity. Education should provide students with the moral equipment to make reflexive judgments as to which choices to take—that is, to make choices in such a way as not to harm themselves and others.

Consider yet another example of a neutral approach to information—genetic counseling. Genetic counseling is commonly defined as giving to individuals and families involved with a genetic disease information about the disease itself, and about the probabilities that their own offspring would be affected by the disorder, so that such individuals can make an informed decision in the planning of their families. One of the basic assumptions of genetic counseling is that the counselor should be neutral in the sense that he or she should not direct the counselee toward any course of action. It is up to the counselee to make up his or her mind on the basis of the information provided. What is totally ignored is that the process of communication in counseling is not just the transmission of information from one who knows to one who does not know. It is a two-way process in which both participants learn more about themselves and about each other in a truly Hegelian manner. Counselees do not accept neutral facts at their face value but interpret them according to their own understanding, biases, and emotions. In no sense do counselees simply assimilate neutral information; they learn facts that concern them, and thus these facts are loaded with emotions, and their acceptance and interpretation may lead to anxiety and feelings of helplessness or relief. In addition, in spite of his or her attempts to be neutral, the counselor, as a reflexive agent, cannot avoid communicating his or her own values, attitudes, and beliefs nonverbally. Thus, the counselor communicates his or her own views by tone of voice, by what he or she does and does not say, or even by choice of words. For example, there might be a psychological difference between formulations such as "there is a 50 percent chance that you will have a healthy child" and "there is a 50 percent chance that you will have an affected child," although from the point of view of the truth-value approach these two formulations deliver the same facts.

Discussing the problem of neutrality in counseling for the amniocentesis of mothers who are at high risk of having Down's syndrome children, Kessler points out that in such counseling a common practice is to show the prospective mothers pictures of Down's syndrome children, photographs of chromosomes, graphs, and so on. As Kessler says,

> this practice is based on standard pedagogic techniques, and, on the surface, appears to be consistent with the neutral educator model of genetic counselling. But such practices may unintentionally focus the counselee's attention on the likelihood of having a defective child rather than a normal one, and, cognitively, magnify their risk for an affected child. Thus, the practice may serve as a means of arousing their anxieties, fears, or aversions regarding human defects and possibly increasing their motivation (or triggering motivation) to take appropriate actions to avoid such a problem. From that perspective, the practice might be interpreted as an attempt to influence the counselees to utilize the prenatal diagnostic procedure, violating professed values of neutrality and nondirectiveness.[30]

Several researchers have recently pointed out that, while there have been rapid advances in human genetics and in its technological aspects, the application of moral values to the possibilities opened up by this new technology is still an area of ignorance and unmet needs. There is a tremendous gap between knowledge of the biochemistry of genetics and associated technological advances on the one hand, and the lack of reflexive thought and morality with respect to these issues on the other.

These examples of assumed neutrality and impartiality with respect to the acquisition of knowledge bring several issues into focus. First, knowledge and morality are still conceived as independent of each other, both in general and in higher education. This, of course, is not to say that education is more guilty of the present state of affairs than the community at large. It is still generally believed that concern with morality should be left to families and churches while education should aim at intellectual achievement. Second, as I have argued, knowledge gained through action transforms the self- and other-awareness of the knower. However, a greater part of the message from television, advertisements, and the popular press is of reward effortlessly gained rather than of human achievements obtained through sacrifice and hard work. Consumption rather than creativity appears to represent the value of the day.[31] In contrast, the evidence of great literature, psychological research, and individual personal experience all clearly demonstrate that commitment to practical issues in the community and involvement in moral action lead not only to a greater level of maturity but also to deeper levels of self- and other-awareness. Helping the suffering and those in need enables one to develop an empathic and caring attitude toward them. The more the effort one puts into one's deeds the more one values one's achievement resulting from such deeds. In its extreme, staking one's own life, the highest value one has, tests one's self- and other-awareness to its limits.[32] Third, reflexivity, as I have already argued, means standing back and interpreting and evaluating the past. In this sense the past may provide one with security for the present and for the future. The past, both one's own and that of the culture in which one lives, enables one to develop self-identity. The importance of one's awareness of one's identity cannot be overemphasized. There are numerous examples of adopted people or of people who have lost their parents and who make tremendous efforts in order to find out "who they are." Loss of memory means the loss of self-identity for the individual, and loss of trust in one's own and of one's sociocultural history means a loss of self-identity. Unfortunately, a historical perspective in university teaching an emphasis on cultural heritage are not among the priorities of present higher education. Efficiency, and short-term and immediate effects emphasizing usefulness and direct applicability, are preferred to reflexion and evaluation of the likely long-term consequences. A historical perspective of a subject not only teaches one to recognize the importance of the effort of past generations but also enables the young to put their own efforts into perspective and conceive of themselves as part of the joint effort of the social group and culture to which they belong.

In conclusion, although the universities and colleges do not determine moral values and norms as such, they can, in a variety of ways, take the leading role in transmitting reflexive awareness with respect to moral values. Although this will require a great deal of imagination on their part, they should aim at providing a light through these difficult times and preserving the human spirit.

Notes

1. Georg W. F. Hegel, "Philosophy of Spirit," in *Gesammelte Werke*, vol. 8 (Heidelberg: Verwaltung des Osswaldischen Verlags, 1805–6), 215.

2. Martin Buber, *The Knowledge of Man: Selected Essays*, trans. Maurice Friedman and Ronald Gregor-Smith, ed. Maurice Friedman (London: George Allen and Unwin, 1962), 68.

3. John O. Lyons, *The Invention of the Self: The Hinge of Consciousness in the Eighteenth Century* (Carbondale and Edwardsville: Southern Illinois University Press, 1978); I. S. Kon, *Otkritye Ja (Discovery of the Self)* (Moscow: Politzdat, 1978); R. D. Logan, "Historical Change in Prevailing Sense of Self," in Krysia Yardley and Terry Honess, eds., *Self and Identity — Psychosocial Perspectives* (Chichester and New York: John Wiley & Sons, 1987).

4. Julian Jaynes, *The Origin of Consciousness in the Breakdown of the Bicameral Mind* (London: Allen Lane, 1976), 75.

5. L. J. Stone, *The Family, Sex, and Marriage in England, 1500–1800*, abr. ed. (London: Weidenfeld and Nicolson, 1977).

6. Elizabeth L. Eisenstein, *The Printing Press as an Agent of Change: Communications and Cultural Transformations in Early Modern Europe*, 2 vols. (Cambridge and New York: Cambridge University Press, 1979), vol. 1; and Eisenstein, *The Printing Revolution in Early Modern Europe* (Cambridge and New York: Cambridge University Press, 1983), 243.

7. David R. Olson, Introduction, in David R. Olson, Nancy Torrance, and Angela Hildyard, eds., *Literacy, Language, and Learning: The Nature and Consequences of Reading and Writing* (Cambridge and New York: Cambridge University Press, 1985), 15.

8. Aleksandr R. Luria, *Cognitive Development: Its Cultural and Social Foundations*, trans. Martin Lopez-Morillas and L. Solotaroff, ed. Michael Cole (Cambridge, Mass., and London: Harvard University Press, 1976), 151–53; Courtney B. Cazden, "Plays with Language and Meta-linguistic Awareness," in Jerome S. Bruner, Alison Jolly, and Kathy Sylva, eds., *Play: Its Role in Development and Evolution* (Harmondsworth, Eng.: Penguin Books, 1976), 603–18.

9. Robert L. Selman, *The Growth of Interpersonal Understanding: Developmental and Clinical Analyses* (New York: Academic Press, 1980); Ivana Marková, *Human Awareness* (London: Hutchinson Education, 1987), 118–27.

10. George H. Mead, *Movements of Thought in the Nineteenth Century*, ed. Merritt H. Moore (Chicago and London: University of Chicago Press, 1936), 74.

11. I. Berlin, "Herder and the Enlightenment," in Earl R. Wasserman, ed., *Aspects of the Eighteenth Century* (Baltimore: Johns Hopkins Press, 1965), 54.

12. Georg W. F. Hegel, *The Phenomenology of Mind*, trans. J. B. Baillie, 2d ed. (1910; London: George Allen and Unwin, 1931), 131–45, 180–213.

13. William James, *Principles of Psychology*, 3 vols. (New York: Holt, 1890), vol. 1.

14. George H. Mead, *Mind, Self, and Society from the Standpoint of a Social Behaviorist*, ed. Charles W. Morris (Chicago: Chicago University Press, 1934).

15. Abraham Flexner, *Universities: American, English, German* (New York: Oxford University Press, 1930), 6–17.

16. Eric Ashby, *Technology and the Academics: An Essay on Universities and the Scientific Revolution* (London: Macmillan, 1963), 4–66.

17. José Ortega y Gasset, *Mission of the University*, ed. and trans. Howard L. Nostrand (Princeton, N.J.: Princeton University Press, 1949), 51–65.

18. Immanuel Kant, *The Metaphysical Principles of Virtue*, part 2 of *Metaphysics of Morals*, trans. J. Ellington (Indianapolis and New York: Bobbs-Merrill, 1964), 12.

19. Georg W. F. Hegel, "The Spirit of Christianity and Its Fate," in T. M. Knox and R. Kroner, trans., *G.W.F. Hegel's Early Theological Writings* (Chicago: University of Chicago Press, 1948; Philadelphia: University of Pennsylvania Press, 1971), 182–300.

20. Ibid., 191.

21. Georg W. F. Hegel, "Love," in Knox and Kroner, trans., *Early Theological Writings*, 304.

22. Hegel, "Spirit of Christianity," 224–25.

23. Cardinal [John H.] Newman, *On the Scope and Nature of University Education*, Everyman Edition (1852; reprint, London: J.M. Dent and Sons, 1915), xxxiii.

24. W. Moberly, *The Crisis in the University* (London: S.C.M. Press, 1949), 22–23.

25. See, for example, Derek C. Bok, *Beyond the Ivory Tower: Social Responsibilities of the Modern University* (Cambridge, Mass., and London: Harvard University Press, 1982).

26. Ortega y Gasset, *Mission of the University*, 78.

27. Ibid., 58.

28. Moberly, *Crisis in the University*, 71–88.

29. Ibid., 53.

30. S. Kessler, "The Psychological Paradigm Shift in Genetic Counseling," *Social Biology* 27 (1980): 167–85.

31. See the essays by Kaplan and Billington in this volume.

32. Hegel, *Phenomenology of Mind*, 234–40.

EDUCATION AND
SOCIAL MORALITY

4

Bruce C. Hafen

ALTHOUGH THIS ANTHOLOGY is concerned primarily with the link between social morality and higher education, some of what I wish to say assumes that we might profitably consider also the links between social morality and the entire American system of education. Higher education, after all, is but the most advanced portion of a vast collection of public and private educational enterprises. Moreover, today's widely expanded access to higher education makes it likely that attitudes and practices in higher education will affect and be affected by attitudes and practices throughout the public and private school systems. We might even decide here that higher education could make one of its most meaningful contributions to American social morality by giving encouragement and leadership to the development of personal, institutional, and social morality in the primary and secondary schools. My references to education will thus usually mean our entire educational system, of course including higher education.

I wish to suggest only the germ of three ideas for consideration:

Bruce Hafen is the former dean of the J. Reuben Clark Law School at Brigham Young University and is currently the provost of Brigham Young University.

1. That we encourage both public and private schools to maintain what I believe is a desirable kind of tension between value-laden and value-free approaches to education, rather than expecting public schools to be only value-free and expecting private schools to be only value-laden;

2. That we think of public schools as institutions that "mediate" between the individual and the state, rather than thinking of the schools only as state agencies; and

3. That we retain a sense of moral idealism balanced with a healthy respect for the limitations of reality, rather than letting our fear of hypocrisy drag us beyond realism into pessimism.

I first wish to describe a relatively recent development in the relationship between public and private education. Imagine two circles of the same size. One circle represents the historical tradition of private education; the other represents the tradition of public education. For many years, these circles substantially overlapped, because they shared much common ground in the educational philosophies they represented. Despite differences in emphasis and degree, the two traditions each maintained a dual commitment to both intellectual rigor and morality. Education in the private sector, especially in religious schools, has tended toward a value-laden orientation; but most of those institutions still maintained a deep respect for free academic inquiry. Their faculties knew that students must discover and assimilate even value-laden truths for themselves, if those truths are to have lasting meaning in the students' lives. The spirit of the Inquisition had no place in this educational vision, because that spirit stifled the internalization of personal virtues as well as it stifled the quest for scientific understanding.

Public education, on the other hand, naturally placed its primary emphasis on the fundamental importance of open inquiry and the assumption of multiple paths to educational truth. The doctrine of separation of church and state as well as the obligation of public schools to an increasingly diverse constituency have reinforced the sense of neutrality inherent in the public schools as state-sponsored institutions. Yet the public-school tradition, reflected in everything from the copybook headings to the pledge of allegiance, also historically included a commitment of respect for the importance of both

character development and civic virtue. The idea that educ[?]
essential to the theory of democracy depended in no small p[?]
assumption that education would aid the development of t[?]
sonal abilities and attitudes. Thus, despite our society's gradually
decreasing homogeneity, the private and public traditions have long
shared a common ground and the mutual respect borne of commitments to both moral and academic principles.

In recent years, however, these two circles have tended to pull
apart, with the common ground becoming more narrow and the
mutual respect between the two traditions eroding in some cases into
bitter mutual suspicion. Some members of the public now want little
to do with the grand tradition of liberal education, as they increasingly identify those who cherish liberal education with what they
pejoratively call secular humanism. Meanwhile, some defenders of
the liberal tradition react to the tradition of moral education with
shock so visible that the two circles seem to have no overlap at all. For
example, Yale president Bartlett Giamatti's letter to his college freshmen in the fall of 1981 deplored the "spiritual violence" of a "self-
proclaimed 'Moral Majority,' " whose "new meanness of spirit" and
the "resurgent bigotry" threatened all traditional educational values.[1]

James Billington has described what I believe to be this same phenomenon: "We are seeing a growing split between those who are
morally concerned but are not intellectually trained and those who
are highly articulate but [seem to appear] morally insensitive. That is
very serious for democracy."[2]

The reasons for a development of this complexity cannot be
explored fully here. But I note in passing my agreement with legal
studies professor Stephen Aarons's observation that the court-ordered
removal of "religious teaching and observance" from the public
schools since the early 1960s has apparently been followed by the
unnecessary and at times unwitting removal in many schools of an
entire range of "beliefs, commitments, and passionately held values"
underlying "the most enduring questions of civilization and human
nature." This constitutional overkill was not mandated by the courts
but was assumed to be the logical extension of the reasoning behind the religion cases by many "citizens, school officials, and teachers wary of . . . conflict . . . that might breed trouble." And, notes

Aarons, the resulting "frustration some families feel . . . has been energetically exploited by the predatory politicians and electronic preachers of the New Right."[3]

I acknowledge the conflicts and tensions that can arise between the intellectual and the moral dimensions of a complete perspective about education. To avoid such uncertainties and frustrations, and sometimes simply to avoid criticism from constituents whose vision is too narrow, some educators emphasize one dimension to the exclusion of the other. That is both unnecessary and unwise. I believe the two circles I have described could return to being much closer together, restoring the educational balance in both the public and private sectors, even while leaving each sector its own understandable emphasis as each school or school system may choose to define it.

I wish to suggest a second historical perspective that is particularly relevant to the way we have come to view public education since the beginning of both school desegregation and the religion cases. Under our theory of constitutional democracy, the state is not the source of the substantive values that give meaning to individual lives. Subject to certain limits at the extremes, state structures and constitutional protections are largely a means toward the end of personal self-determination. Yet the influence of the state has become so pervasive today that its silence on many personal value questions is perceived by many to create something of a value vacuum.

Richard Neuhaus and Peter Berger have thoughtfully described the interactive relationship that exists between the public and private spheres. The personal, private sphere is where "meaning, fulfillment and personal identity are to be realized" in one's life. The public sphere, which by their definition includes the institutions of the economic marketplace as well as the institutions of government, is made up of megastructures that are "typically alienating . . . [and] not helpful in providing meaning and identity for individuals' existence."[4] Standing between the individual and the megastructures are such "mediating structures" as families, churches, and voluntary associations. These mediating structures are said to be "the value-generating and value-maintaining agencies in society."[5]

For example, the family is "the major institution within the private sphere, and thus for many people the most valuable thing in their lives. Here they make their moral commitments, invest their emotions, [and] plan for the future."[6] Thus, the family interposes a significant legal entity between the individual and the state, where it performs a mediating and value-generating function. We fully expect parents to relate to their children in ways we would not tolerate from the state; namely, the explicit transmission of intensely personal convictions about life and its meaning.

Parents have therefore enjoyed the constitutionally protected right to direct the rearing and education of their children. The schools— public or private—to which parents sent their children were thus traditionally regarded as *in loco parentis,* meaning literally in the place of the parents. In this sense, both private and public schools originally assumed a mediating structure role as extensions of the family.

In more recent years, especially since the schools were called upon to assume a primary role as direct state agents in the desegregation of society, the structural place of the public school system has become less clear. What is a public school today? Is it an extension of individual families and therefore part of the value-oriented private sphere? Or is it an extension of the state, which would make the public school part of the more value-neutral megastructure? Clearly the public schools today are by law and in practice primarily extensions of the governmentally sponsored megastructure. However, many parents and others still assume that the public schools should play a value-transmission role more typical of a mediating structure. The reality is that a public school is now cast in both roles, with its newer tradition imposing a form of value neutrality while its older tradition asks it to play a parental role—teaching a basic sense of right and wrong along with teaching civic virtue. This structural ambiguity has become a source of tension and ambivalence in the minds of teachers and administrators as well as in the public's perception.

This recent movement by the public schools away from the role of mediating structure toward the role of megastructure is actually quite typical of the way public perceptions and legal attitudes toward other mediating institutions have been changing. The momentum of the individual rights movement has placed such an emphasis on individual claims that virtually *all* institutions are seen as threats to personal liberty, whether or not they are part of the constitutionally limited megastructure. This institutional perspective on public schools has also undermined their mediating role.

It is ironic that the admirable sense of social morality that fueled the school desegregation movement may have eroded in this way the functioning of public schools as extensions of parental influence. I am not convinced, however, that public education is today simply a bureaucratic arm of the state having no serious mediating function to perform. The schools still have a unique role to play in fostering and developing the individual values on which the fulfillment of democratic theory depends. For instance, our schools should be considered primary sources for teaching the values of free expression that underlie the First Amendment. The intellectual development nurtured by good education can be critical in helping the young learn to participate meaningfully in the marketplace of ideas.

When education is seen in this light, the courts should be more willing to defer to school administrators' judgment about the content of either the student newspaper or the nature of a school's teaching about civic virtue and discipline. An educational institution should thus enjoy its own kind of First Amendment protection for the purpose of developing students' capacity for both responsibility and free expression. That is the proper role of a mediating institution, which the schools for some purposes should continue to be. Part of our challenge may be to clarify those purposes.[7]

I wish to mention briefly a third recent development that occurs to me in part because of the fears Robert Coles's essay expresses about the risks of hypocrisy. Our society has been undergoing a subtle but important shift in understanding the meaning of moral discourse, as we have moved from a morality of aspiration toward a morality of the practical norm. Max Weber once distinguished between these two different levels of moral expectation in these words: "All systems of ethics, no matter what their substantive content, can be divided into two main groups. There is the 'heroic' ethic, which imposes on men demands of principle to which they are generally *not* able to do justice, except at the high points of their lives, but which serve as sign posts pointing the way for man's endless *striving*. Or there is the 'ethic of the mean,' which is content to accept man's everyday 'nature' as setting a maximum for the demands which can be made."[8]

American society's attitudes have been somewhat cyclical in moving back and forth between the idealistic standard of the heroic or aspirational ethic and the more realistic standard of the ethic of the mean. Since our disillusionments of the late 1960s and early 1970s, however, we seem to have embraced the ethic of the mean more fully than ever before. As we have collectively lost confidence in our ability to practice what we preach, our sense of disappointment has moved us to find another sermon. Now we prefer to preach whatever we happen to practice. That is an instantly successful antidote for guilt.

This recent shift is easily illustrated in the tones and themes of our movies, television programming, and popular literature. Law professor Carl Schneider has pointed it out clearly in American family law,[9] where our once idealistic attitudes toward divorce, spousal support obligation, and sexual behavior outside marriage have given way to a set of legal norms symbolized by the very term "no-fault divorce." We are no longer comfortable with Max Rheinstein's observation that our earlier laws were written idealistically enough to keep the conservatives happy but were enforced realistically enough to keep the liberals happy.

There is some truth behind Rheinstein's general assumption, however, that a little hypocrisy is not all bad. We have always known — and still know — that there is an inevitable gap between the *is* and the *ought*, between our realities and our aspirations. Whether the gap is good or bad is partly a matter of attitude; that is, whether we view the gap as a source of debilitating frustration or productive striving.

I detect in the prevailing contemporary attitude, especially among the highly educated, not only disdain for aspirational morality but at times downright embarrassment. Having successfully convinced the emperor that he wears no clothes, some realists wish now to rejoice in his nudity. Imagine their disgust, then, when some thoughtless idealists still call out slogans celebrating what a lovely plaid outfit he is wearing. As an alternative to both of these extremes, I would prefer a candid acknowledgment of the nude emperor's need, followed by a trip to the nearest clothing store.

Whatever we make of an invitation to reconsider the place of aspiration, I hope at the least that we are not embarrassed by it; for if we are, our doubts can weigh us down enough to assure the victory of pessimism. I seriously question the value of endless and superficial moralizing about morality, but I also share philosophy professor Christina Sommers's concern about college professors whose uneasiness about aspirational morality develops into such deep doubts that they have "a principled aversion to the inculcation of moral precepts."[10] C. S. Lewis understood this problem and responded in this way:

> [Many college professors] see the world around them swayed by emotional propaganda—they have learned from tradition that youth is sentimental—and they conclude that the best thing they can do is to fortify the minds of young people against emotion. My own experience as a teacher tells an opposite tale. For every one pupil who needs to be guarded from a weak excess of sensibility, there are three who need to be awakened from a slumber of cold vulgarity. The task of the modern educator is not to cut down jungles, but to irrigate deserts. The right defense against false sentiments is to inculcate just sentiments. By starving the sensibility of our pupils, we only make them easier prey to the propagandist when he comes. For famished nature will be avenged, and a hard heart is no infallible protection against a soft head.[11]

To illustrate how educators' fear of hypocrisy can immobilize them, I quote the words of a high school drug counselor to educational researcher Gerald Grant, who asked whether the counselor directly approached the students known to be drug users. The counselor said: "Let's face it. It's not a problem if there is no effect on the kid's performance. I mean, who are we to say what's right or wrong? A kid could always turn around and say to you, how many of the faculty have an alcohol problem . . . ? And yet their job goes on, they continue to teach—they can point that out to you. So who are we to say what's right or wrong?" Citing this as a typical example of "the collapse of adult authority as representing a standard for children," Grant concludes that public school students and teachers "no longer have any agreement on what . . . morality ought to be or [we] feel that any attempt to provide it is a form of indoctrination," because we are "declaring—even insisting—that children are adults capable of choosing their own morality as long as they do not commit crimes."[12]

It seems to me that we can and should seek a vibrant balance between aspiration and reality, not by the naive belief that we can easily close the gap between the two, but by the informed belief that humankind's endless striving toward an ever-receding ideal is the fundamental energy of human progress.

I conclude with my view that higher education does have a role to play in stimulating the moral life of our communities. I do doubt the wisdom of a university's taking positions on social and political issues, not only because politicization compromises higher education's basic premises, but also because I agree with Christina Sommers that this emphasis suggests to college students that morality in "modern life is mainly a question of learning how to be for or against social and institutional policies." This attitude places students in "the undemanding role of the indignant moral spectator."[13]

Higher education might help respond to the evidence of declining commitments of discipline among our young people, just as it has responded to the national decline in academic achievement — by asking in a leadership role that students bring better preparation with them to college. Such expectations might earlier have seemed inconsistent with the focused role of a university on intellectual training, but, as Dallin Oaks has noted, "the soundness of that approach depends upon the reality of its assumption that someone else will teach the values essential to the preservation of our nation."[14]

Today's problems with student behavior in the public schools do suggest an usually high need for help. Of course these problems may be largely the result of weaknesses in family life and other social and economic structures. But that does not make the influence of educational institutions irrelevant. Even if educational influence accounts for only a fraction of the variance among other causes, more effort is justified. Moreover, the public visibility of educational effort just might encourage more attention to matters of value and character elsewhere in society.

I believe that the development of personal character (which, in the aggregate, is the ultimate source of social morality) is more a matter of skill development and attitudes than it is a matter of learning information. It is probably best taught, therefore, in the master-apprentice relationship of a close child-parent tie or in schooling from especially devoted teachers. Due to the mutual respect that characterizes such relationships, the master can make demands of the apprentice, the justification for which the apprentice may not at first comprehend. There can also be supervision of practice and, hence, learning through trial and error.

Unfortunately, American parents increasingly seem to doubt that their children require such arduous education, whether at home or at school. Indeed, it has become fashionable to regard children on a kind of quasi-adult level that liberates them from the demands of old-fashioned morality on the simple grounds that kids are people too. I note the irony, however, that this parental attitude also serves the convenience of parents who prefer a less encumbered life-style.[15]

It does seem natural for education to play some role in encouraging the familial and social patterns in which apprenticeship morality is learned, because that learning is, after all, an educational process. If higher education can do little else, it might begin by teaching its students something about being parents and by helping the public schools develop more confidence in both their right and their need to develop relationships of aspiration and apprenticeship with their students.

Notes

1. *New York Times,* Sept. 6, 1981, sec. 11, p. 25.

2. *U.S. News and World Report,* Oct. 1, 1984, p. 70.

3. "Commentary," *Education Week,* Nov. 7, 1984, p. 24.

4. Peter L. Berger and Richard J. Neuhaus, *To Empower People: The Role of Mediating Structures in Public Policy* (Washington, D.C.: American Enterprise Institute for Public Policy Research, 1977), 2.

5. Ibid., 6.

6. Ibid., 19.

7. For a more extended treatment of the theme of public schools as mediating institutions, see Bruce C. Hafen, "Hazelwood School District and the Role of First Amendment Institutions," *Duke Law Journal* (1988): 687–705, and Hafen, "Developing Student Expression through Institutional Authority: Public Schools as Mediating Structures," *Ohio State Law Journal* 48 (1987): 663.

8. Letter to Edgar Jaffe in 1907, quoted in Carl Schneider, "Moral Discourse in Family Law," *Michigan Law Review* 83 (1985): 1803, 1819.

9. Ibid.

10. Christina Sommers, "Ethics without Virtue," *American Scholar* (1984): 381–82.

11. C. S. Lewis, *The Abolition of Man* (New York: Macmillan, 1947), 24.

12. Gerald Grant, "The Character of Education and the Education of Character," *American Education* 18 (1982): 135, 143, 146.

13. Sommers, "Ethics without Virtue," 388–89.

14. "Presidential Leadership and Commitment to Values," in *Higher Education: The Job Ahead* (Rexburg, Idaho: American Association of Presidents of Independent Colleges and Universities, 1982). Dallin Oaks, formerly a President of Brigham Young University and member of the Utah Supreme Court, is now a general authority in The Church of Jesus Christ of Latter-day Saints.

15. For some additional development of this theme, see Bruce C. Hafen, "Exploring Test Cases in Child Advocacy," a review of *In the Interest of Children: Advocacy, Law Reform, and Public Policy,* edited by Robert H. Mnookin, *Harvard Law Review* 100 (1986): 435, 445–49.

Walking a Certain Fine Line

5

Robert Coles

I WAS A COLLEGE STUDENT after the Second World War. In many of my classes I felt like a small child. Sitting next to me were men who had fought in the jungles of far-off Pacific islands, or on the blood-soaked fields of France. They were in their middle twenties. A number had been decorated. Many had seen their close friends killed in action. Some had been wounded themselves. Now they were going to classes and at night retiring to dormitories, where they studied, talked, tried to figure out where they wanted to go next (those long bull sessions students frequently have). Those veterans also wanted to entertain their girl friends in their rooms, or take them to supper in a college dining hall. One of them became a roommate of mine during my sophomore year. He was twenty-five, had lost an arm, and had several times narrowly escaped death fighting on an island named Guadalcanal in the South Pacific. He had met a woman, a nurse at the nearby Massachusetts General Hospital, and he wanted her, occasionally, to cross the Charles River and visit him in Cambridge. She did so, but they had to be very careful about their watches—set them and make sure they worked—because in Adams House, where we lived, and in all the other "houses" or dormitories, there were "parietal

Robert Coles teaches at Harvard University.

rules," which determined how long, on which days, "guests" (meaning girl friends) could be entertained. The usual length of those "parietals," as I remember, was two hours—from five to seven in the evening. At any moment before or after those hours, one or another college official (the house superintendent, one of his assistants, this or that junior faculty member) might knock firmly on our door, come in (whether asked or not), look around until his curiosity was satisfied, then leave.

I have clear memories of some of those visits—the utter silence as we were searched, so to speak. I also have clear memories of what my roommate felt, and, occasionally, said to me and his girl friend as we hurriedly left our suite at, say, one minute before seven. I have an especially clear memory of what happened one evening—at two or three minutes after seven—when he and his girl friend and I, having left our room at seven sharp and gone downstairs to have supper, were told that we couldn't have that supper, at least in our house's dining hall. We had both forgotten to wear our ties; and jackets and ties were *de rigueur* then, morning, noon, night. When I had forgotten my tie on other occasions, I'd had to climb the four flights to our top-story place to fetch one of those striped jobs, which I wrung haphazardly around my neck. But this time we'd arrived at the very end of the dining-room hours, which ran, in fact, quite precisely parallel to the parietal hours: five to seven. No point in trying to hurry back up those stairs, we were told: the place was closing up. So, we left quietly, retired to a nearby eatery, where my roommate ordered a beer for himself and his girl friend and one for me—even though, unlike them, I was under twenty-one, the age of permissible drinking. It was then that my roommate, an English major and an eloquent talker when he wanted to be, began a memorable diatribe against college rules and regulations, against an enforced manner of living which (so he felt) demeaned him and those keeping their eyes on him.

We didn't have tape recorders then—the early 1950s—and even if we had been able to record his oration of sorts, I surely would not have chosen to do so. Why bother, when his words were being insistently offered to us two listeners, and when our ears worked well, and our brains, too: we could get his message loud and clear and not easily forget it. I may not have every word right, but I'll dare paraphrase him, even today, with the conviction that I'm doing his message no injury: "I'm sick and tired of this place! They treat me as if I'm a boy. They're poking around—*assuming the worst*. Here I am, over twenty-five, my left arm gone, and a battle scar on my right upper leg, and still with some stomach trouble from a parasitic disease I got in Asia, and I have to sit and stare at the clock with one eye while I'm looking at my girl friend with the other eye, because it's five of seven and there might be a knock on the door. And a half hour ago, because we forgot our ties in our rush to clear out of the room, we lost a chance to have a meal paid for at the beginning of the term, two months ago—and tonight I'm violating the law by getting a beer for you. What does all this prove?"

He went on to mention Perry Miller, whose course "Classics of the Christian Tradition" we were both taking and enjoying enormously. A week or so earlier Miller had given us a lecture on the New England Puritans. In the course of the lecture he commented on the slow attrition of once firmly held moral principles in early nineteenth-century Massachusetts—the collapse, really, of a way of life as a nation began to grow commercially and as its secular values exerted a gradually increasing tug on even avowedly religious men or women. He interrupted that historical account to suggest that we, too, might soon enough be witnesses to a significant moral shift of sorts. A world war had ended; a once established European order was in shambles. Moreover, our own country now had unprecedented power and responsibilities—and was on the verge, it seemed, of giant strides economically. Consumers were asking for more and more, and the Depression, with its austerity and melancholy, seemed even then to be fading from the memories of millions of people. Such political and economic expansion would prompt social and cultural changes—and moral ones, too, he had remarked.

His words were echoing in our ears as we contemplated the parietal rules. Even as Professor Miller had witnessed the horror of the concentration camps during his stint in the American army in Europe, my roommate's closest friend at Harvard, also a veteran, had been at one of those camps, a member of an American "skirmish patrol," he called it, that stumbled into such hell on earth one day in the spring of 1945. Now, five years later, that former soldier, a college undergraduate like my roommate, in his middle twenties, had to keep his eye on the clock when he entertained a friend in his room. All of us that evening were wondering what our responsibilities and obligations were, never mind those of our Harvard teachers and administrators. "I can take care of myself," my roommate had often said. He had already read a bestseller titled *1984*, which had come out two years earlier, and remembered that phrase "Big Brother": to him—a man who had, indeed, proved himself able to take care of himself—college officials were such "big brothers."

To be sure, the immediate response of some of us will be that such a time was special, that such undergraduates were quite special. Yet, they did not feel, then, that they were entitled to a special dispensation, as a tribute to their extraordinary status as Harvard undergraduates who also happened to be, often enough, war heroes. (My roommate had been twice decorated, and several others I knew in Adams House had also been honored with one or another citation by the government.) Rather, my roommate kept on arguing (that night and on other occasions) a different proposition: we who lived in the house were adults and should be treated so. One day he took several of us with him to see the house master, David Little, in order to argue his case in the strongest possible language.

How well I remember that rainy October afternoon! The storm lashed at the windows of the house master's office, even as my friend and roommate spoke his remarks with great force and eloquence. Frankly, at the time I was in awe (and anxiety) not only of what he said and how he said it—but *that* he did. No wonder I remember the weather! I was brought up by parents who taught their children to be quiet, reserved, compliant to authority—a teacher's, an institution's; so much so that, when I became involved in the civil rights movement of the early 1960s, I can recall my father (and he was far from alone, then) expressing his dismay at the student-sponsored sit-ins and picketing. The courts should be the avenue of protest, he earnestly believed. Students ought to study. Students ought to think about social and political problems, true; but street demonstrations, disruptions of life's everyday rhythms, confrontations, marches—they were the stuff of social disorder, unnecessary and undesirable in a democratic society, so he averred, and especially if students are leaving their libraries for such activity. As for a "protest" in the name of a suspension of parietal rules, or a change of rules with respect to the wearing of a necktie–my parents would never have believed that I'd even have entertained such an idea, let alone followed it through and taken the step of accompanying my roommate, who had become to me a figure *in loco parentis*.

My roommate had been studying moral philosophy and would eventually write a long essay on Dietrich Bonhoeffer–his theology and his struggle against the Nazis, culminating in his death in a concentration camp shortly before the end of Hitler's rule. My roommate couldn't seem to get out of his mind what had been seen by those of the American Third Army who liberated Buchenwald. Then and there in Adams House that concentration camp scene, and indeed the Holocaust itself, seemed to be coming to his mind, and through him to the minds of the rest of us–my other roommate, the house master, and his discreet but attentive administrative assistant, who had a way of keeping watch over all of us, we had learned. The gist of what that veteran of battle had to say went something like this: Why is Harvard singling out us undergraduates for the kind of moral scrutiny we were getting–rules about how we dressed and how long we spent in our room with our girl friends–when there were plenty of other people in the world, even some connected to Harvard, who deserved far closer moral scrutiny than us undergraduates?

He didn't only ask in so many words such a question. He hastened to give us a series of speeches, interrupted now and then by the house master. The two of us who were his roommates sat utterly still–to be honest, frozen with fear and the developing confusion that set in as we heard the discussion develop. I now realize that the subject of "moral education" was really the topic of our roommate's lengthy speeches, which at one point the house master called "a series of disquisitions." They were, in fact, passionate statements–from a war veteran who had tried to learn some lessons from his military experience. To this day I remember his challenges to us in that room–and, indeed, only recently shared them, yet again, with the Philadelphia Coordinating Council on the Holocaust at their annual conference (November 10, 1986). He reminded us of the educated ones, the intellectuals who had embraced the Nazis early on–the professors, the doctors and lawyers, the prominent military and business figures. He reminded us how slow, how very slow the churches were to oppose Hitler—how many members of the religious communities in Germany (and Poland and Austria) embraced Nazism. Who is fit to preach to whom about what? Whose hands are all that clean? Moral education for what purpose—so that students will be more circumspect in their rooms and with respect to beer (or, these days, drugs), yet continue to push and elbow and slam their way ahead, not all that concerned about others elsewhere in the world (indeed, elsewhere in Cambridge, Massachusetts) who are living exceedingly difficult lives, who exist at the very edge of things? Who is teaching a practical social ethics to college teachers, to college administrators—so that they are held to account not only for their words, but their everyday lives? (He quoted to us Perry Miller's remark one day in class: "The Harvard Faculty Club has more than its fair share of strutting peacocks.")

Those (paraphrased) questions were a bit truculently put to a rather kindly and sensitive Harvard official, himself a living refutation of what our roommate was asserting with respect to a given college and, more, all institutions of higher learning. I suppose if I were the psychiatrist then that I am now I'd have been all too tempted to turn on the fellow, call him some thinly disguised psychological names—dismiss him as in need of "help." Psychiatry, in that regard, as the Soviets have discovered, can be a great boost to the keepers of a social or political order's keys, can help buttress normative standards with the imprimatur of supposedly medical nomenclature—no matter that psychiatric labels and categories are all too readily applied or avoided, in keeping with the subjectivity of the particular doctor in question. Those I "like," or whose attitudes I favor, tend to get one kind of description, and those whose manner or background I find uncongenial, or even threatening, quite another.

At that time, however, there wasn't the extensive "mental health" clinic we now have at Harvard. Somehow, we all muddled through or, alas, failed to do so. My roommate never had his mind questioned psychologically, as I remember. The house master listened attentively to him, told him he admired his spunk displayed that afternoon, even as he admired his awesome military record. He also told him—told us—that he agreed that Harvard could most certainly be occasionally a rather hypocritical place but that such a distinction did not uniquely belong to it. The world is full of hypocrisy, pretence, phoniness, two-faced characters of one sort or another, liars, and frauds—some of them living out lives as college officials or teachers, admittedly, and others as "members of government" or, yes, ministers. Still, we were reminded, to be eighteen, say, is not to be twenty-eight or thirty-eight. "You will admit that our freshmen—save you who have come here as veterans, a special case—are nearer to adolescence than our graduate students or our junior faculty." I think those were just about exactly the master's words—and I recall the outburst they prompted; our roommate's derisive reminder that eighteen-year-old men had been fighting a war and were quite honorably able to acquit themselves in that regard. As for the moral life of those called elder statesmen, who had in various ways over a generation or more of time contributed to the development of that war—well, the mere mention of that irony was enough to bring our roommate to a pause.

I refer back in time to those moments in an undergraduate career because they turned out to be morally edifying for the three of us in Adams C-45. A few days later we brought elements of our Adams House meeting with the house master to class, so to speak—discussed yet again those same issues in Perry Miller's class. He was one professor who wasn't only interested in the study of moral philosophy through abstract analysis. He was forever reminding us that ideas and ideals don't necessarily translate into conduct—that one can study (or teach!) moral reasoning, and do a brilliant job, and still be a first-class scoundrel with respect to the way one lives one's personal life. I mention the great philosopher Heidegger's infatuation with the Nazis, and Jung's similar spell of friendly association, or the sad personal life of the sensitive and discerning theologian Paul Tillich, as described by his wife in an autobiographical account, not in order to single out such important intellectual figures of this century for special attention or animus. I happen to admire aspects of each of their thought; and I was a student of Tillich's—a grateful and admiring one. As a matter of fact, I took his seminar in systematic theology at Harvard, while a psychiatric resident in 1957, and found him gracious and inspiring as we discussed the very issues my roommate had brought up a few years earlier. Tillich managed to read each of the essays we wrote for him. He had put a big question mark along the margins of mine, written on the subject of "practical ethics"—how one decides that the way one is living one's life is just and in keeping with the teachings of the Hebrew prophets, Isaiah, Jeremiah, Amos, and the instructions of Jesus of Nazareth as embodied in the so-called Beatitudes, or Sermon on the Mount. I wondered when I saw that question mark, in black ink, what he had in mind—a questioning of my mode of thinking, or an attempt to indicate his own perplexity in the face of one more student's interest in posing impossibly demanding quandaries? At the end of the essay he was a bit more forthcoming, however. "If we would all practice what we preach, the world would be a much finer world. Who of us ever does, completely?"

That (second) question mark was smaller—but, of course, much bigger, because it had been accompanied by a revered and wise teacher's humble, even confessional disclaimer. After all the hours of complex theology, we had come down to a homily of sorts—the kind of aphorism, actually, a George Eliot or a Tolstoy, in their romantic idealization of the peasantry, might have summoned or appreciated. Yet, once one turns from theology (or the construction of the novels which make up "literature" or "the humanities," or, yes, "the Western moral tradition") and reaches for the common verities—then, what of the obligations of professors or college administrators with respect to the conduct of their students? My roommate's major point was that his lived life was a fairly good match for that of the various authorities whose job it was to watch over him. Because he was a war hero, we all quaked in our boots as he spoke—I think even the house master. A professor (Perry Miller) supported his thesis. "We are walking a certain line," he told us in class one day—and spelled out his notion of the desirable geography on both sides. On the one side there should be respect of teachers and students for each other, and a reasonably well-ordered climate of behavior in classes and in dormitories—with no one hurting others; and on the other side there should be a willingness of college officials to treat students as fellow citizens, as reasonably sane and competent adults—who, after all, are old enough to go fight for their country and (these days) vote, and hold elective office, and, in general, be considered full-fledged adults.

Still that "line" of Miller's shifts about, as the years offer new worries, new concerns, new opinions (and not least, new political constructions of moral and social reality). We ought to remember what Philippe Ariès told us in *Centuries of Childhood*—that for generations people only old enough by our lights to be considered "children" were regarded as adults who worked and bore adult responsibilities. In the course of my work with migrant farm families and other quite hard-pressed and vulnerable families I have met boys and girls in America who are, for all practical purposes, on their own: working in the fields, traveling with crew leaders, spending what little money they earn as they please, and not subject, really, to anyone's moral supervision. On the other hand, a recent *Wall Street Journal* article tells us that in England "many young adults live like eternal adolescents." On and off the dole, constantly preoccupied with certain consumerist obsessions, they seem the polar opposite of the children Ariès describes; and much of their manner of living is sanctioned by the government itself. Who is to keep watch on their personal lives, decide about the rights and wrongs of their manner of living— these "children" (are they?) or youths (are they?) or adults (are they?) of, say, twenty-five or thirty or forty?

Sometimes when I watch or hear of students in one or another college committing pranks, or involving themselves in bullying politics, or getting stupidly drunk or high, or behaving promiscuously—hurting themselves and others with their assertive sexuality— I wonder whether there isn't something people like me (the so-called older generation, and their teachers) ought be doing to encourage more "maturity" in "them" and to obtain more civility for all of us who live or work on this nation's campuses. Still, as I go from college to college to give speeches or take part in meetings, I am struck by the thoughtfulness and sensitivity and kindness I find in so many, so very many, of the students I meet. Surely some of us know of all too many instances of wrongdoing, personal or professional, among college teachers or administrators: sexual misconduct, alcoholic excesses, serious sins of omission and commission, not to mention the episodes of mischievous gossip or slanderous rumor-mongering or wicked bad-mouthing—with, sometimes, so-called tenure up for grabs under such less-than-honorable and indecent circumstances. The worst sin is the sin of pride, the Bible tells us—and in that regard, our students may need a few more years (and some coaching from us) to catch up.

Before I wrote this essay I made it a point during my office hours to talk with students about the general question of what role a university ought to have in the collective moral life of its students. Again and again the students—men and women, politically "liberal" and politically "conservative"—stressed the importance of a kind of education in which "the idealism in books gets translated into the way we live." I recall the remark of one young man from San Antonio, Texas, who was at pains to let me know that he was tired of seeing professors give lectures, then walk away from the moral matters they mentioned until the next lecture, even as he abhorred a similar inclination in students. He wanted a "social morality" alright—a world in which teachers and students alike not only *professed* high-sounding ideas but tried to live up to them. He happens to be a student—to make matters as complex as so often they are in real life—who does a fair amount of drinking on certain occasions, has used pot now and then, *and* who works long and hard at tutoring poor children who live not all that far from Harvard Square. Indeed, he spent one summer doing so—lived in a housing project where he worked full-time at such tutoring. I do not feel that I am the one to take an inventory of his sexuality or his possible involvement in "substance abuse." I can picture in my mind some young man, somewhere (in Cambridge, for instance) who won't go near drugs, won't touch alcohol, and does quite well in his school subjects—and doesn't have the slightest interest in any poor and troubled children anywhere. I think St. Paul did well to remind us in his Second Letter to the Corinthians: "not of the letter, but of the spirit" (3:6), and indeed, "not in tables of stone, but in fleshy tables of the heart" (3:3).

To stay with biblical imagery, we ought be quite careful lest we forget to ask ourselves who, indeed, ought be casting stones at whom—lest we, blind in our own ways, lead blind others by virtue of a moral authority we claim for ourselves but may not earn in our daily lives. As I look at the likes of certain well-known contemporary (political) ministries, hear and see the preachers on television, listen to them worrying about America's young—oh, I wish for them a mirror and a fervent moment of Augustinian self-scrutiny.

What precisely ought to concern us about our college-attending youth? I would hope that we would encourage them to think of other young people, the world over, not so lucky as to be going to our many and fine colleges, and not with the bright prospects our students have. I would hope that we would encourage those students, also, to think about not only themselves and their future, but others, in cities or sections of cities nearby, who might be given a beckoning nod—so that most of us would want to try to be of help, we who have no small amount of luck in our corner.

Without question we all ought to be asking ourselves what our moral responsibilities are—to one another in our particular community, but also to others in communities near and far. We ought to be doing so, I hope and pray, not in self-righteous smugness, in exaggerated excitement and alarm (which serve to divert us, sometimes, from other possible lines of moral inquiry), but with a certain sense of historical proportion—remembering, for instance, the terrible moral excesses and the terrible narrowness and arrogance of past generations of students and teachers alike during those "good old days"!

We should, finally, remember that "walking a certain fine line" can very much be a moral contribution in itself—to sift and sort, to weigh judiciously this side of things and that side, to resist the blandishment of a particular headlong rush inspired by a particular historical moment's "principalities and powers." The universities—places in which many matters are constantly being considered, and presumably places with a good sense of time past and time future, as well as time present—ought to be in their sum the last territory to yield eagerly to a yahoo morality that would shape people up, have them reciting certain pieties, yet fail to inspire in them and their teachers alike the kinds of searching ethical inquiry I remember that roommate of mine making over a quarter of a century ago. Indeed, speaking of Jim, I now realize how much I was in awe of him years ago. Here was someone who had faced down danger, put his life on the line for his country, found in himself bravery, courage, no matter the inevitable anxiety and fear of combat, the instinct of survival most of us have all through our lives. Here was someone who may have been injured, may have lost a limb, yet he had gained something precious, something not all that common—a sense of who he was, what he could be and do, a capacity for wry observation of others, and most impressive of all, a certain confidence in himself: I have faced down death on a distant battlefield, and so I can surely deal with the small banalities, if not idiocies of everyday life here, whether those demonstrated by Harvard bureaucrats or any other kind. Jim had endured pain and loss, but he had gained a moral and psychological perspective on himself and on others that many of us surely lacked then, and may not ever have acquired all these years later.

He is now, by the way, a medical missionary in Latin America—and rather more worried about other aspects of American moral life than that of the character of its college student population. He worries about our Ivan Boeskys, about our longstanding coziness with the likes of Pinochet, about the crying poverty he sees every day, while billions and billions of dollars are earmarked for bloated and even bizarre military expenditures. He worries about his own beloved Christianity, too. He worries about the lip service so many of us pay to a particular religion, while the moral example of the way Jesus lived his life—with whom he spent time, and his messages rendered again and again in his parables and sermons—all get somehow forgotten or are not permitted to engage with our daily experience. I think of that old roommate often as I hear certain big shots worry about the moral life of our nation's young people. I wonder why it is that lives such as his, values such as his, aren't worked into an ongoing life, honored by more of those who are wringing their hands publicly about the matter of "morality" on our campuses.

One way to do so—bring the values of such a life to our universities—would be to design courses that take up directly the moral questions encountered by those who do community service. Where better to discuss the intellectual and emotional matters which volunteer activities generate in young people—the enlightenment they experience, the frustrations, disappointments, the moments of achievement, the times of melancholy? Need community service be an altogether separate activity—unconnected to the ongoing intellectual growth of students? Students of mine who both tutor children or work in soup kitchens and read certain novels, stories, journalism, and social science texts of related interest find themselves thereby awakened all the more not only to what needs to be done, but what they as individuals might do—a worthy beginning, indeed.

On the Moral Responsibilities of Universities

6

Noel B. Reynolds

WARNED BY THE DANGERS of such a vague and elusive topic, one might be more prudent to take the easy way out. After all, is it not obvious that moral responsibilities are the property of individual human beings and not of institutions, which are in a real sense abstractions? But the experience of our times teaches us that there is a great deal at stake in this discussion. As universities everywhere are plagued by the compromises brought on by departmental fragmentation and government regulation, we need new and stronger insight to help us in the critical steps ahead. To the conversation that is emerging on this issue I here recommend both a perspective and an analytical structure that I believe can help us, one, understand better that universities do indeed have important moral responsibilities, and, two, see what those responsibilities imply for the conduct of university administrators, faculty members, and students.

Noel B. Reynolds is a professor of political science at Brigham Young University.

The Economic Perspective:
The University as an Asset in Human Capital

A university is a capital asset of rather impressive proportions. When people first visit a university campus, they are invariably impressed by the vast array of specialized buildings, all equipped with the elaborate paraphernalia of research and teaching. They see libraries everywhere and an endless collection of computers and other high-technology devices. But as important as all this is to the effective conduct of university work, there is an intangible, almost invisible element to this capital asset which dwarfs the physical asset in its importance.

A strong university cannot be created overnight with money alone. Even if you could provide all the necessary buildings, books, and equipment and bring in a high-quality faculty, it would remain to be seen if a good university would result. For a university exists primarily as a complex set of expectations established between people, expectations which are built up over time as people pursue learning in a community context.

These expectations include the understanding of the university's mission, the standards of individual moral conduct, the standards of performance, the level of commitment to the pursuit of knowledge, and the policies and procedures by which the institution and the individual members of the community will guide their conduct. Such expectations grow up over time. They are healthy and strong to the extent that individuals have chosen to commit themselves to establishing high levels of mutual expectation and to the extent that such choices have been reciprocated throughout the community as a whole. They are weak or of reduced value to the extent that individuals are not interested in the university as a whole but only draw from its strength and use it as a resource for their personal efforts.

It is this set of expectations which I see as the most important capital asset of a university. No one from the outside can give a community this kind of capital. It must be built up through the contributions of countless individual community members over long periods of time. And it can be diminished significantly or even destroyed in short periods of time by thoughtless or selfish individuals who carelessly or maliciously attack or undermine the understandings and expectations on which it is built.

Because this kind of capital is built of the higher dreams and aspirations of men, which transcend or even conflict with the narrow pursuit of individual interests, it is not possible for a strong university to develop or continue where a shared community vision of the university mission is lacking or confused. This principle seems to explain what I have seen at Harvard, Edinburgh, and Brigham Young, the three universities that I know best.

The one year I spent at the University of Edinburgh as a visitor put me in a good position to observe some of that institution's distinctive purposes and functions. The University of Edinburgh is one of the grand old universities of the world and during the eighteenth century enjoyed the distinction of being possibly the world's best. Part of the distinctive set of expectations that define its mission are derived from its geographical location. Because of the nature of the British union, the people of Scotland have retained a lively concern for the preservation and understanding of their Scottish heritage, a tradition which appears on every hand to be endangered by the dominant English culture. To an outsider, the university exists at least to some extent as the citadel of Scottish achievement. Edinburgh sponsors possibly the strongest programs anywhere in Scottish history, philosophy, languages, literature, religion, and law. It has recently completed an extraordinary international celebration of the eighteenth-century Scottish enlightenment, which has led to a significant revival and renewed appreciation for the achievements of a past heyday. The university obviously seeks excellence in all the areas of study one would find in similar institutions south of the "border." But it also obviously invests considerable resources in studies that are quite particular to the Scottish cultural and religious heritage. In a time of budget reductions, this no doubt looks to some like an expensive luxury. But to turn away from this aspect of its unique mission would signal betrayal to the majority of the supportive community.

Because of the distinctive religious character of its mission, Brigham Young University affords me another dramatic example with which to illustrate my point. Brigham Young University has experienced the same evolution in mission that has occurred at hundreds of other nineteenth-century academies that have grown into full-scale universities in this century. But even that process of transformation has been guided by aspirations and commitments arising from a unique vision that originated with its earliest founders, faculty members, and students. This vision is based squarely in an understanding of man and his relationship to God that derives from the restoration of the gospel of Jesus Christ to Joseph Smith over a century and a half ago. It is quite simply this vision of a new Christian revelation that has given this university community its sense of identity and mission and gives its members the possibility of rising above themselves in building a community which can serve as a rich resource to men and women from all the world who desire to seek truth and knowledge aided by the particular light this revelation gives. Almost any university has its own stories of people who have been guided by some vision of the preeminent value of education and who have made the necessary sacrifices to enable the institution to survive crises and grow stronger over the years. Some of those visions are religious; others are secular. In either case, these particular understandings and aspirations will have shaped curriculum, faculty selection, and procedures, giving the institution a peculiar identity and mission.

It is for this reason that members of any particular university community cannot attack or undermine the validity of its inherited vision without attacking and undermining the central capital of the university community. The vast network of commitments and standards on which the community has been built are tied directly to that understanding. Because communities rest on complex accretions of reciprocal expectations, the beliefs, attitudes, and ideas held by individuals can determine the fate of the community. The core of expectations that defines other more secular universities may not be so distinctive as the example described above. But it seems to me to be just as important to each of them, and to be just as much in need of respect and protection. And the widespread movement to jettison the guiding visions of the past in pursuit of some elusive national model has created a good deal of confusion and loss of direction on many campuses.

But even universities in transition must recognize as a minimum that a university is a community of trust. No university can endure while failing to recognize certain universal expectations. No one will steal another's work or ideas. No one will promote views that have not or are not being subjected to critical scrutiny. No one will allow the interests of the university to be sacrificed for lesser and non-academic reasons. These are part of the internal morality of all universities, regardless of idiosyncratic backgrounds, which morality is discussed more fully below.

Any community rests on basic moral expectations that define the way in which individual members are to be understood and treated. This morality sets limits to acceptable behavior at the same time that it outlines shared aspirations. The traditional morality shared by universities includes recognition of each community member as a rational and responsible agent committed to the pursuit of truth and virtue. In past centuries it was usually assumed that these two pursuits were one because God was the source of both. In a largely secularized twentieth century, attempts have been made to separate these pursuits, though it would not ordinarily be accepted that a university could have as a fundamental purpose the pursuit of truth with the intent to do evil.

A university community requires continuing investment, not only of financial resources but of human effort. Unless there is widespread dedication to intelligent study and investigation of ideas, a university community will decline. Students can only discover the value of learning through association with teachers who are also learning. This generation cannot afford to communicate to upcoming generations that the present state of knowledge is adequate or that they should be satisfied with what has been learned to this point. In all matters—in our understanding of the world, of man and society, and of our God—there is so much that we do not fully understand. It behooves us to be humble and open and diligently engaged in pursuing greater knowledge.

A community is a shared enterprise and prospers to the extent that each member contributes to building up the common resource. One who isolates himself from the common aspects of the enterprise draws from the common resource as a parasite, taking but not giving. If some choose not to give of their time to build the common resource, or hold and spread attitudes that destroy the community base, others must sacrifice at a higher level in order to strengthen and maintain the institution, or the institution will go into decline. Each serves most importantly by doing his or her own job well. But each must also contribute by working positively on committees, giving extra support to students, and encouraging adherence to the highest standards in all that he does and to all with whom he associates.

Members of university communities observe a range of attitudes in the colleagues that surround them. I personally came to university life without any developed concept of what a university was or of the community that is required to make it work and prosper. But, over the years, I have learned much from others, mostly older than me, who had caught that vision and who were willing to make the investments from which the rest of us were benefitting so greatly.

THE ANALYTICAL MODEL:
UNDERSTANDING INSTITUTIONAL RESPONSIBILITY

We hear much about the responsibilities of universities in a world where there is less and less agreement on moral questions. But we have difficulty making sense of the competing accounts of the problems and possible solutions. Much of the confusion which characterizes these discussions can be resolved by clarifying what we mean when we say universities have moral responsibilities. I propose that our expectations correspond to the various modes of action available to these institutions. And these modes include much more than corporate faculty actions. Universities act in a corporate capacity when their most authoritative officers set policy or implement programs, or fail to do the same. At the individual level, universities act when a faculty member or officer carries out some university function or performs a service, or fails to do so. When we speak of university responsibilities, we refer to a wide range of expectations we hold of the institutions, their faculties, and even their students. Such expectations, legitimately held against universities, constitute moral responsibilities of these institutions. But ultimately it mostly comes down to expectations about what officers of universities should and should not be doing in their capacities as faculty members and administrators. Though it is often more natural to speak corporately, as language naturally invites us to do, when pressed we can explicate an institutional responsibility in terms of the responsibilities of the individuals we identify with the corporation for any specific purpose that may be relevant.

The External Morality of Universities

One might reasonably ask why anyone should have a right to expect anything of universities beyond the normal kinds of contractual and statutory obligations that any corporation incurs. Indeed, universities constantly generate large numbers of standard contractual obligations—with students in particular. These responsibilities of universities are articulated and standardized in the opinions of courts that hear suits against them. And universities are learning to be careful in documenting their deliberations and decisions with respect to the progress of students, who might later find reason to sue the institution for negligence or abridgement of certain rights. Faculty concerns such as hiring, firing, promotion, and affirmative action have been even more extensively litigated.

But does this exhaust the responsibilities of universities? One set of answers to that question is derived from the community purposes universities are designed to serve. Communities large and small have come to support thousands of universities in recent centuries, with some common purposes in mind. Central to all these purposes is the provision of an institutional means of educating the rising generation in the wisdom of the past. The highest achievements of our cultures and of our civilization are embodied in our art, literature, and science, in our philosophy, in our public institutions and laws, and in our history. Yet it is not an easy matter for young people to master these on their own, or even with inexpert help. The accumulated literature of our civilization is large and complex. Any systematic attempt to master it, or even to gain passing familiarity with it, is facilitated by the tutelage of learned individuals who have dedicated their lives to its study. There is a great efficiency in bringing students and scholars together in institutions dedicated to the transmission of this cultural heritage to new generations.

Extending the knowledge and understanding gained in the past constitutes a second major purpose. The same individuals who have prepared themselves to teach the new generation are in the optimal position to criticize and extend that tradition through the development of their own insights. But such creative efforts require significant concentration and investments of resources. Institutional support is crucial. Consequently, universities have emerged in our society as one of the principal means for assaulting the boundaries of the arts and sciences. Much of the funding now channeled into universities is earmarked for the advancement of knowledge. Universities operate on the assumption that faculty research activities will also improve their value and effectiveness as teachers. Research and other creative activities provide professors with insight and understanding transcending what they could get through mastering the ideas of others. And it also helps them develop a commitment to learning that makes them personally more effective and interesting.

There is a third, and perhaps nonessential, function that has been superimposed on universities, determined perhaps by the economic character of human life. Every society faces the task of preparing new generations for productive activity during their adult lives. Because universities already have a developed teaching institution, and because they have the attention of young adults during that period of their lives when they are studying the heritage of the past, they are efficient providers of specialized training in the skills that are demanded in the marketplace. Families are no longer as effective in this function as they once were. Young men no longer learn the basic productive skills they will need from their fathers; young women increasingly want to learn productive skills unrelated to the domestic functions filled by their mothers or grandmothers. There is thus a strong market for effective education in such skills; and universities, particularly in America, have rather naturally stepped forward to meet the need. It must be remembered, however, that this additional purpose can compete negatively with the other two. Though all of the three purposes outlined above are potentially competitive with each of the others, the natural mutual reinforcement between teaching and research does not occur with skills instruction. It requires thought and care for a university to integrate the three functions smoothly and without compromises that undermine the performance of one or more of them.

Another form of the moral responsibilities that belong to universities arises from their universal dependence on external communities for support. Support is provided in many forms, but always on the basis of certain expectations which are affirmed or legitimated by the acceptance of the support. These expectations are in turn based in certain understood central functions which the universities are thought to serve, including education in significant cultural traditions, research and the expansion of the arts and sciences, and training in productive skills. The foregoing list indicates five ways in which university administrations, faculties, and students incur a form of moral responsibility to their larger communities to promote these basic understood functions. There may be other important functions not mentioned, and there may be other forms of support not listed. But this brief account should be adequate to establish clearly the basic outlines of strong forms of responsibility that the students, faculty members, and administrators have toward their external supporters.

The external dimension of the responsibility of universities is not determined exclusively by investments of money and other resources. By the mere fact that they exist, universities by default inherit a range of community expectations that might be met in other ways in other societies. Communities have no other way to communicate their highest cultural achievements and understandings systematically to those who will be the cultural, economic, and political leaders of the next generation. A university occupies a privileged position in a community partly because of the expectation that it will fulfill this role. To fail to do so would violate those unavoidable and legitimate expectations.

Graduates of universities in general provide the pool from which our leaders in all aspects of community life will be selected. Their ability to lead us effectively, taking advantage of past achievements and avoiding past errors, will be largely a function of the quality of the understanding they have of those achievements and errors. Their sense of responsibility in community decision making can be enhanced by an appreciation of the tenuous nature of past gains.

Universities are uniquely placed to have opportunity to teach these future leaders how to think honestly and clearly, how to deal with problems in an intelligent and responsible way without resorting to unexamined ideologies or prejudices. A failure of the university to cultivate thinking skills in students and faculty is a lapse in its community responsibility. And the university carries this responsibility largely by default. There are no other institutions in modern societies that can fill this function for this critical age group.

These common purposes ascribed to universities account for the different kinds of community support they receive. And that community support, based on community expectations derived from these purposes, translates into responsibilities that universities have to the community. The following breakdown of the ways universities and faculty members depend on community support demonstrates how fundamental and extensive these responsibilities to supporting communities can be.

1. Universities as a whole have a strong responsibility to serve the common good of the larger community. One can hardly imagine a university that is not dependent for its very existence on the support of a larger community through taxation, donations, tithes, tax breaks, and the like. Few institutions of higher learning are able to maintain a significant university program purely on the basis of tuition. This means that the larger community purposes which induce legislatures, churches, corporations, and private individuals to support universities impose legitimate expectations on universities that accept this support. That many of the moral responsibilities of universities trace back to this expectation created by university reliance on community financial support is further discussed below.

2. Because good universities are the product of investment by previous generations and because that cumulative investment is essential to the development of such an institution, each university has a set of inherited expectations to meet. Certainly a university is not shackled to every dream of its past supporters. But to the extent that there is a core of constant and recognized expectations that have evolved through the years, the institutional officers risk betraying a great deal if they arbitrarily shift directions or abandon significant commitments which have been important to past gen-

erations of supporters. Managing a university is a trusteeship function. A university is a community possession that can only fulfill its purposes across many generations. The university never belongs to the officers of the institution at any given point in time, even though they must bear the responsibility of making significant decisions for its future.

3. The faculty members of a university, like even larger numbers of their counterparts in society at large, have acquired extensive obligations through the investment made in them by universities and university supporters in the past. Few holders of the Ph.D. can say they have paid for their own education. Even full tuition payers are heavily subsidized at most Ph.D.-granting institutions. Accepting such support over the years creates a legitimate expectation that the recipients will act to fulfill the purposes for which the support was given, which in a broad sense are the general purposes for which universities are supported. Who can feel morally comfortable with a colleague who has accepted such support over the years and who is not in agreement with the underlying purposes of such institutions?

4. Faculty members acquire additional levels of obligation as they use university support for their research and their careers. The cash payment a faculty member receives each month does not constitute all that the university provides for her. Rather, she is the beneficiary of all kinds of support and facilities which are provided with certain general expectations in mind. Without the layers of institutional support faculty members take for granted, most of their important research work would not be possible. Accepting that support generates legitimate expectations. Government research support presents an ambiguous case. It is often provided without restrictions. But national interests must eventually be recognized if Congress is to be accountable. Academicians need to be wary of funding that might compromise the integrity of their work. But they cannot simply assert the right to do whatever they think is right, regardless of the expectations of the providers of the funds.

5. Students likewise acquire obligations when they accept the highly subsidized education that universities offer. Again, this obligation

can only be understood in terms of the common good of the community and the expectations underlying the giving of support to universities.

The Internal Morality of Universities

Can we say anything about the responsibilities of universities, as discussed above, other than to identify the implications for various members of the community? Examining the separate functions of universities more closely, we will find that they each require certain minimal practices or policies for their achievement. Because these policies are implied in the function itself, I refer to them as an *internal morality* of universities. Without some support for these policies, a university cannot accomplish its essential purposes.

For example, the nature of learning and research as human endeavors forcefully imposes its inner logic on universities. To the extent universities can be legitimately expected to promote learning, this must be done in the ways that learning is best accomplished. A university obviously has by extension a responsibility to foster a healthy learning environment, within the limitations of the resources available to it. Once one thinks about this it becomes apparent that there are certain things that universities should and should not do, just because of the nature of their primary function.

1. University functions and curriculum must not be politicized. Learning requires the kind of thinking which is protected from insistent outside demands for decisions and action. University experience of the past two decades makes it clear that there are plenty of people who would like to capture the resources of universities for the advancement of their political causes. Without attempting to judge the merits of such causes, it is clear that a university can become party to such activities only at an unacceptable cost to its fundamental mission and in violation of the expectations the larger community rightly has of it.

2. The production and communication of human knowledge is a social process. Most of what is known at any one time is a gift from past generations. A healthy learning environment is one in

which the gains of the past are energetically maintained and used in building for the future.

3. Human understanding is finally holistic. We naturally try to fit all we know and believe into a single integrated view of reality. A healthy learning environment will encourage the development of the whole person and not allow the educational process to get out of balance. A single disciplinary point of view will not be allowed to drive out all others.

4. Universities have an inherent responsibility to help students with their moral thinking precisely because a university education unavoidably contributes to the unsettling of values and models of the world that students bring with them from their childhood. These models and values must be reexamined from an adult point of view. But to encourage this in the absence of strong support for the reconstituting of an adult commitment to appropriate values is inexcusable.

Reason does not demonstrate the self-sufficiency of reason. It ill behooves academics who do not have irrefutable answers to these questions to attack or ridicule the answers that young people may find attractive. Because it is not humanly possible to demonstrate rationally the correctness of any religious or moral outlook, the best we can do is to compare different possibilities in the light of our experience and limited understanding. The moral and religious beliefs of any human being may be both precious and fragile. Their value to the individual may be infinite. University professors must conduct themselves at all times in such a way that they do not destroy what they cannot rebuild.

5. A university is an institution whose possibility assumes certain relationships between belief, knowledge, and truth. The idea of a university assumes that the human pursuit of truth can bear fruit, that there are truths to be learned which are not determined by irrational or arbitrary accidents of history or nature, and that such truths are worth the effort it requires to learn them. There are ideologies among men which deny this linkage between beliefs, knowledge, and truth. For them to claim to have a knowledge of truth would be a self-contradiction. Certainly a university must provide opportunity to its students and faculty to learn about such

views and study them in detail. But it cannot be other than a failure of purpose for a university to allow itself to be dominated in its decision-making processes by people who deny the possibility of those pursuits to which universities are committed. Subversion is a possibility in all communities, including universities. To allow or encourage it is a betrayal of the trust that universities unavoidably hold.

The foregoing account of an internal morality of a university indicates some of the ways in which the most fundamental purposes of universities dictate a set of minimal policies and practices. The short list given here is not intended to be exhaustive. I explain below how both the external and the internal responsibilities of universities can be translated into the moral responsibilities of specific people.

Understanding the Corporate Language of University Responsibility

To this point I have employed the fiction of the corporate responsibilities of universities without specifying how these translate into real individual responsibilities. But critics of such holistic talk are surely correct in saying that it is meaningless if it does not "cash out" in terms of individual applications. To meet that criticism, I now propose to specify how the moral responsibilities of universities translate into the moral responsibilities of trustees, administrators, faculty, and students.

The *trustees* often bear the direct responsibility of mediating between community and university interests. Theirs is the task of monitoring the university's activities and the extent to which these match the support community's expectations. In this sense, they are the watchdogs of the university mission.

But the trustees cannot be unsympathetic toward the university faculty and administration in their attempts to realize that mission. It is essential that there be a close working relationship and understanding of how that mission is to be pursued, so that the trustees can be energetic and effective in securing to the university the ongoing support that will be needed. Wise trustees will recognize that a university will be most effective when allowed a considerable latitude to define its own programs, and that there will be some failures. Not only do trustees bear a burden of trust, but they must demonstrate trust toward the people they choose to lead the university community.

The *administration* is usually drawn from the faculty and is closely identified with it. But the moral responsibility of the university often devolves on the administration differently precisely because of its unique functions. In contemporary universities, some of the most significant responsibilities borne by administrative officers arise from the universal emergence of departments as centers of power and decision making. The tendency of this new breed of department is to put departmental interests above university interests in hiring and curriculum decisions. If a university is nothing more than a collection of departments, an administration may find itself merely managing the allocation of resources. The growing prominence of this model among American universities is one of the chief reasons that the present topic is coming to the fore. Who in such a university is looking out for the responsibilities of the institution as a whole?

In general, the answer to this problem is the institution of meaningful university-level review of departments. The goals of a particular university and the moral responsibilities of all universities combine to provide standards for such reviews. Hard decisions about budget and curriculum can be linked to reviews that hold the same high standards out to every department, giving them the real incentive to become all that they can become. Departments have a natural incentive to do well that comes from participation in the discipline itself on an international level. But this is often not enough. And there are fields of academic study which do not police themselves well. National professional organizations will not take much initiative to reform an occasional backsliding department. It is unfortunate that these associations sometimes take positions designed to prevent universities from bringing professional departmental programs into line with the university mission. It is the inescapable responsibility of the university administration to be on top of this situation, to reward and support departments that are doing well, and to encourage and educate those that are not. And in all this, the administration can extend the vision of university-level responsibilities and standards that the departments should be including in all their deliberations.

The dominance of the department in most universities is what lies behind the last decade or two of concern about the decline of general education and the liberal arts. As departments focus increasingly on narrow areas of research expertise and expand course requirements in the major, departmental resources and student time available for traditional general education subjects are squeezed ever smaller. And because general education is not seen to benefit more than a few departments directly, it has tended to receive lower priority than the ambitions of the more technical and specialized departments. In this circumstance, a university administration has the opportunity and the responsibility to take a firm stand and provide strong leadership in educating and uniting the departments of the university in support of the institution's broader responsibilities. Leaving the defense and leadership of general education to key departments in the arts and sciences makes it into a departmental interest, to be weighed in alongside all the others, and will lead to its demise. Leaving it to departments to determine which of their courses are suitable for general education credit invites them to be judges in their own cause, especially where enrollments are linked in any way to other resources. Again, the administration must provide university-level faculty review of departmental participation, insuring uniform standards of general education throughout the university curriculum.

The university decision which most affects the ability to meet larger responsibilities is hiring. Contrary to what is often said, and probably even believed, the entire university has something at stake when a department hires a new faculty member. The new member may be called upon to teach general education courses or to serve on university committees or in administrative positions. Every newly hired faculty member will be called upon to express opinions and assist the department and the university in the pursuit of their missions. Hiring procedures need to reflect that university interest, or it will not be possible for the institution as a whole to be effective in the fulfillment of its larger responsibilities. Again, failure to see this explains much of the recent decline in universities' ability to meet those responsibilities.

In my experience, Harvard University provides an outstanding example for all others in this principle. As I understand the procedure, the departments appropriately take the lead in identifying suitable candidates for open positions. However, the criteria used, even in the first instance, have a strong university component. The department eventually forwards its recommendation to the dean, accompanied by confidential statements from each member of the department faculty. If the dean supports the department proposal, he can in turn propose to the president that the candidate be hired. At this point, the president assembles a special committee which is dominated by faculty members outside the department and even outside the university. Thus, the dean and the president, at their respective levels of review, bring university-level interests and views to bear on every proposal for hiring in tenure track positions.

The administration controls the university facilities and the policies governing student and faculty conduct. It is at this level that the most effective steps can be taken to guarantee a healthy learning environment on any campus. Insisting on putting education first and on maintaining high standards of conduct and mutual respect between members of the university community all contribute to the effectiveness of the institution in pursuit of its mission. Toleration of behavior that demeans others or the educational process will undermine the ability of the institution to meet its moral responsibilities. The administration must take the lead in university discipline and mobilize the support of the faculty and the students in that effort.

In any university the *faculty* is the major key in these matters. If a faculty cannot govern itself well and accept the full responsibilities that fall upon it and the university, there is little the administration or the trustees can do to overcome this failing. On the other hand, a strong and enlightened faculty can hardly be prevented from carrying out the mission of the university, even in times of weak university administration. What is needed is that each member of the faculty understand the sense in which a university is a community with significant responsibilities transcending departmental boundaries. By taking this into account in the carrying out of her personal assignments and responsibilities and when participating in institutional decision making, she can so act that the larger mission of the university is promoted and protected.

There are common patterns of behavior which betray the failure of a few faculty members to catch this larger vision and which constitute violations of the moral responsibility they bear in their university roles. Using a university position or resources for political activism is fortunately much less common today than a decade or two ago. Using professorial skill or authority to subvert or even attack the beliefs or integrity of a student or colleague also violates proper conduct. Failing to adhere to high standards of teaching excellence and commitment to the pursuit of knowledge is always a possibility and must be resisted with the greatest determination. Faculty members have a moral responsibility to the community not to become tired, lazy, or indifferent with respect to these matters.

There must be a defensible distinction between political activism and standing squarely for one's values. One of the naivetes of our positivist century is the widespread view that we can teach without reference to our beliefs about the things which matter most. The moral stance of a teacher is important to her students, no matter the subject of the course of study. And in many subject areas, the political convictions of the instructor will also be relevant. Students do not expect professors to be agnostics in these matters. And it is far easier for the student to understand what is being taught when he knows where the professor stands. Open confession in this sense promotes the essential functions of the university without distorting them. Academic freedom is rightly understood to include protection for the profession of personal beliefs.

The distortion witnessed in recent decades occurs when small groups of self-appointed agents of social and political change seek to capture the resources and the machinery of universities as a means of advancing their views, without respect for the legitimate expectations of those who establish, build, and support universities. There are regimes in the world which consciously support universities as instruments of social and political change. But in free societies where universities are most often based on conservative principles which respect the achievements of the past as the appropriate foundation for future building, insider attempts to manipulate the institution to serve a radical agenda must be seen as subversive relative to the mission of the institution. It is a misguided notion of academic freedom which protects subversion of academia.

Students have been known to act as though only the faculty and the administration bear significant moral responsibilities. But as the foregoing analysis demonstrates, students too are the beneficiaries of major community support. And additionally, at least in selective universities, each student holds a seat that someone else would like to have. This is only a problem when the one holding the seat fails to use the proffered opportunity responsibly. The highly supported time set aside for learning is sacred, though this may be hard for students to understand. They can be more responsible in their positions if they are encouraged by teachers and others to respect learning and to give their own studies the most serious effort of which they are capable. To do less is to compromise that portion of the moral responsibility of the university that falls to the students themselves.

Even the *nonacademic staff* of a university, often ignored in this kind of discussion, have significant opportunity to contribute to or detract from the university's fulfillment of its moral obligations. Not being academicians themselves, it is sometimes harder for staff members to appreciate fully the priority that must be given to the learning process and to the protection of a learning environment. Confronted by the idiosyncrasies of a particular faculty member, student, or administrator, it is not always easy for a custodian or secretary or even admissions officer to act in full support of the university mission. But their actions will nonetheless have some impact on the institution's overall ability to acquit itself well.

I have argued that the corporate approach to discussing the moral responsibilities of universities can be reduced to the responsibilities of individuals who are members of university communities. Those responsibilities arise externally in terms of the universities' dependence on and derivation from a supportive community and internally from the nature of the learning process itself. Meeting those responsibilities requires appropriate conduct on the part of all members of the university, from the trustees, the nonacademic staff, and the students to the faculty and the administration. And failures of a university to comply with its moral responsibility can be explained in terms of the failures of some of these individuals.

The intangible complex of human expectations that has grown up in any university community may constitute its greatest asset and, in effect, defines that particular university and its mission. The invisible understandings that exist between past and present university personnel, students, and external supporters are far more important to an effort to understand the moral responsibilities of the institution than are any of its more visible components. Because no living person or group of persons control all those expectations, there are strong limits on what current decision makers can do without violating the legitimate expectations of the larger university community.

Further, the long-term contributions of the larger community to a university generate a set of legitimate expectations which amount to an external moral responsibility for the university. The very requirements of the learning process itself in turn generate an internal moral responsibility for the institution. Against the view that institutions as such cannot be said to have moral responsibilities, I have explained in some detail how these two forms of moral responsibility translate into the specific responsibilities of trustees, administrators, faculty members, students, and nonacademic staff. I conclude that there is a strong sense in which universities have moral responsibilities and that these directly affect the expectations we can rightly hold of individuals in their conduct as members of a university community.

History, Morality, and the Modern University

7

Warren Bryan Martin

THE MEXICAN AUTHOR, poet, and diplomat Octavio Paz writes that "the great wound of the West has been the separation of morality and history. In the United States this division has taken on two parallel expressions: empiricism on the one hand and moral abstractions on the other. . . . The secret of the resurrection of the democracies – and hence of true civilization – lies in the re-establishment of the dialogue between morality and history. This is the task of our generation and the one to come."[1]

Paz believes that certain writers – Max Weber, José Ortega y Gasset, Hannah Arendt, Albert Camus – lived the great breach between morality and history, with some trying to insert morality into history and others trying to deduce from history the foundations for morality. And a few others – Simone Weil, for example – showed through their life and work that morality cannot be divorced from history.

While Paz speaks of writers and their roles, I ask the question: Can the American university today, along with other important institutions such as churches and synagogues, respond to the challenge to reestablish the dialogue between morality and history? Furthermore,

Warren Bryan Martin is a senior fellow at the Carnegie Foundation for the Advancement of Teaching, Princeton, New Jersey.

is there a chance of showing that morality and history must go forward together—in the university as well as elsewhere in society?

To begin the search for answers to those questions is immediately to encounter certain observers who see the university as part of the problem and hence unable to contribute to the solution, because the university is, regrettably, still too tied to its history. That history, these critics assert, is precious, elitist, dysfunctional, and therefore capable of providing only negative lessons for persons who would plan for the future rather than live in the past. Perhaps the time has come, according to this argument, to recognize, if not honor, today's entrepreneurial university. It is an institution living without obligation to history and finding its moral meaning not through ties to tradition but through its contributions to the needs of the moment. Life in this new university is not linear and sequential. Yet there is no embarrassment when things bounce around and shift, or when life within the institution is shaped by environment. No apology is given when faculty members ride off in all directions, given their differing specializations and individual eccentricities. People in physics simply do not need botanists in order to do physics.

This modern university, freed of myth and memory, makes no effort to be a unified community. It features congeries of disparate programs connecting only as clusters of overlapping interests. The closest it comes to community is when faculty members talk about "communities of competence." Nor does this university have one culture. Instead, it has many competing cultures. Remember the differences between residential students, who usually are typical college-age youth gladly immersed in a traditional college culture, and the growing number of commuting students—now 30 percent of undergraduates—who are older, part-time, no-nonsense adults whose primary loyalties are elsewhere.

Why should a university be obligated to its history when that record is burdensome if not downright immoral? Surely, as the entrepreneurial university shows, it can be modern and stand free of tradition. So it is said. Indeed, the same sort of thing is said about modern art. In 1986, at the Pompidou Centre in Paris, there was an ambitious exhibition of sculpture gathered under an equally ambitious title: "What Is Modern Sculpture?" The curator for this show,

Margit Rowell, gave an uncompromising answer. She insisted that "modern" means "belonging entirely to the present and, with no memory and no history, constituting a complete rupture with the past."[2] After seeing this exhibition, critic Robert Hughes wrote, "Modern sculpture after 1910 wanted the liberty that painting had claimed—the unobliged liberty of thought itself."[3]

But does thought ever function "unobliged"—in sculpture, modern art, or the university? More specifically, can higher education have authority without drawing on tradition and history? Answers do not come easily and those we take most seriously are usually unsettling. Here is Hannah Arendt's treatment of these issues: "The problem of education in the modern world lies in the fact that education by its very nature cannot forego either authority or tradition, and yet must proceed in a world that is neither structured by authority nor held together by tradition."[4] Another way of putting Arendt's point is to say that, unless there are accepted postulates in society at large, there can be no compelling postulates to be taught and learned in society's educational institutions.

Steven Muller, recent past president of Johns Hopkins University, has stated his conviction that leadership for education in values cannot come from the modern university, at least until it and society are reformed: "We are very good at training new generations not only to function with what we have discovered but to become discoverers themselves. That's the good news. The bad news is that the university has become godless. We must confront so many value issues, from euthanasia to genetic engineering to weapons that can destroy the world, and we no longer have the strong religious rallying point that we had in the nineteenth century. We have to develop a new value system."[5]

It is this frightening situation, as described by Arendt and Muller, that causes leaders such as William Bennett, former secretary of education, to call for renewed concentration on the "values agenda." Bennett and others insist that there are great value-laden themes— that is, historical values widely shared such as justice, discipline, honesty, courage, responsibility, the pursuit of excellence—that can still be integral parts of the college curriculum. Failing to instill these values means that institutions of higher education, like so many other institutions in society, are reduced to calling on individuals to develop a personal ethic while institutions fall back on the impersonal judgments of the law and the courts. But this course of action too often leads both institutions and individuals to settle for that which is "law honest." There is a story from Puritan history in America that reveals how quickly morality can be circumscribed by this "solution." A New England merchant lived, as was common, over his place of business. One morning before opening the store, he called down the stairs to his apprentice—"Edward, have you put the water in the milk, have you blown up the butter, have you added the chicory to the coffee? Then come on up to morning prayers."

Civilization for the future will surely be less attractive than the civilization of the past unless we can learn from traditional values how important it is to be more than just "law honest." Gerald Grant, professor at Syracuse University, has pointed to the consequences of ignoring tradition and allowing the resolution of differences to be left to the shifting interpretations of law and courts.

> In such a world, even assuming a perfect system of law, where do we develop a sense of discretion about when or whether to sue? For no legal system can stand if all are litigants much of the time. Where do we develop a sense of sympathy? Even when we are right, we should not always press for damages. Where do we develop a sense of integrity? For we can be within the technical limits of the law and without a shred of virtue. Where do we develop a sense of community that maintains us amid the mess and slippage, the horrible contingencies of this life, against which the law offers little refuge?[6]

How can we accept President Muller's challenge to build a new system of values without making reference to existing values, without drawing on the lessons of history and setting our efforts at reconstruction on the foundation of tradition? Consider again that impressive exhibition of sculpture in Paris. Did modernism in art, including sculpture, break completely with the past? Hardly. Albert Elson, art critic, has written: "Modernism has always contained within itself a memory of what was, thus creating the standards that artists either work with or react against."[7] Clearly, the challenge for many modern artists, including two featured in the Pompidou show—Picasso and

Matisse—was how to extend tradition into their own times meaningfully, through changes in degree that finally became changes in kind.

Despite disagreements in society today, most of the citizens are law-abiding even as the communities are reasonably orderly. As John Gardner put it in his 1987 essay, "There are those who believe that any moral order that may have characterized our society has long since disintegrated, but fortunately we are not so bereft. . . . We still have a serviceable framework of values. It is not clear and sharp, but it is there and it prevails a great deal of the time."[8] Gardner becomes more specific about those shared values, and their source, and the responsibility of leaders to serve the areas of agreement: "We must hope too that our leaders will help us keep alive traditional values that are not so easy to embed in laws—our feeling about individual moral responsibility, about caring for others, about honor and integrity, about tolerance and mutual respect, and about individual fulfillment within a framework of shared values."[9]

While the university cannot function any more than society without history and morality, yet, alarmed by parts of its past, it seems to be trying to do so. Whereas, earlier, the chapel and the library symbolized the essential axis on which the university turned—the transcendental and the humanistic, the spiritual and the intellectual—now, on most campuses the chapel seems to be more like a burnt-out volcano. It may once have been at the center, full of light and heat if not fire and smoke. But no longer. It may still be the focal point of campus architecture but certainly not of campus life. At best it is a center for ceremonial occasions—weddings, anniversaries, burials, various campus rituals. As for the library, while it is still featured and often called "the heart of the campus," we cannot claim that the culture of the modern college or university centers on the library—certainly not for undergraduates. It may still be a place where reserved books must be secured by students in order to carry out the instructor's assignment. And the library remains on many campuses a popular social meeting place—quieter and more private than the student union. But most evidence concerning the reading habits of undergraduates stands against the notion that the presence of a library guarantees that a college will have "students of books"—that is, students whose lives are shaped by books—just as evidence makes clear that the presence of a chapel does not assure that the institution has "students of the Book." The library on most university campuses is probably more important to faculty than to students. Indeed, at many colleges as well as universities, the library is organized more for the convenience of faculty than for the needs of undergraduate students, with more money going to buy journals and books deemed necessary for faculty research projects and the work of their graduate students than for the purchase of core readings useful to the general education program.

There is another and related concern. While the library retains at least a symbolic importance, and even financially hard-pressed colleges are still willing to spend ten to fifteen million dollars to erect a new one, the electronic revolution and the emerging computer culture may soon make the library in its brightest expression look and feel much like the campus chapel. Laser printing and other technological developments are greatly reducing the need for vast, repetitive accumulations of books and journals. In the future, regional research libraries will allow many smaller colleges and universities to limit their holdings to basic collections for undergraduate instruction. Certainly it will be hard then—indeed it is hard now—to argue that the library, any more than the chapel, is the heart and soul of the modern campus.

Clark Kerr of California used to amuse his audiences, as did Robert Hutchins of Chicago, by commenting that most universities were held together by their heating plants and parking lots. The British version of this caricature has been that the only thing known about university work was that it seemed to be characterized by simultaneity and juxtaposition. Maybe it is more true now, albeit less amusing, to say that computer networks are the organizing principle for the university. Electronic systems as well as computer networks are emerging as the spine and ganglia of many campuses. The effectiveness of the hardware is currently limited by the ineffectiveness of much of the software, but the future of the "connected campus" seems limited only by the wit and imagination of its creators.

But can the computer culture, as influential as it is or soon will be, hope to compete with that other culture, that other overwhelming force on campus—intercollegiate athletics? It is in the field house and stadium that the college community is likely to come together, not in the chapel or library. Athletic coaches now have more influence with students, and maybe with administrators, than do campus chaplains or people in student personnel services. And the big-program coaches are paid a lot more than faculty or presidents. In recent years, corporate consultants and chief executive officers have been paying as much attention to corporate cultures as they have to such things as sales strategies. They know that strategies can make or break sales. Now they realize that a corporate culture can make or break strategies. By the "corporate culture" is meant the amalgam of assumptions and purposes, myths and rituals, heroes and gurus, programs and "carrying mechanisms" that, taken together, give an organization character and vitality. Is all of this any less true for a college or university? The corporate culture has its equivalency on campus. And one of the tragedies of life on too many campuses is that big-time sports, usually football and basketball, shape the culture, providing the rituals and ceremonies, programs and schedules, heroes and leaders, commitments and sacrifices that give the place such distinction as it has.

All of the criticisms stated or implied in the preceding paragraphs are, I believe, more or less true for most colleges and universities. Leaders in those institutions are often eager to collaborate with forces not only from state and federal governments but also from business and industry, forces that are not only willing to cooperate with them but also to exploit them. Faculty today will sometimes debase their profession by wildly searching for a hot new property—the equivalent in their field to the cabbage patch doll.

Administrators as well as faculty are easily mesmerized by the computer culture and the seemingly endless potential of big computer networks. Universities, as the criticism has it, are opportunistic to a fault. And these intellectual "communities" are, alas, as much driven by emotion as they are by rationality. Large numbers of administrators and faculty, as well as students and alumni, apparently feeling the need for celebration and symbolism, come together at the stadium or in the field house to pour out their emotions with such enthusiasm that sports researchers now solemnly factor in "the home field advantage"—a touchdown in football and five to ten points in basketball.

But having made this acknowledgment, it is also important to emphasize that the university today still struggles amid its many compromises to retain a measure of institutional independence, to bring critical perspective and objective evaluation to the excesses of the very government and those same businesses that help to fund it, to keep its passions under control and to channel its energy and emotion into useful endeavors. A great and significant struggle is going on in institutions of higher education—to assure integrity in scholarship and research even in the presence of evidence showing some tampering with, say, lab experiments and research data. Colleges and universities are also trying to hold the line on plagiarism, among faculty as well as students—and, equally, to protect a good measure of academic freedom, despite some disruption of public meetings on campus and occasional breakdowns in the spirit of civility. Aware of grade inflation, sexual harassment, and any number of other problems, the majority of universities today are still committed to certain enduring virtues—coherence in the curriculum, professional standards for faculty, fair and just treatment for all members of the educational community.

These goals cannot be achieved without drawing on "ideas of value" that have endured, and are still accepted in colleges and universities. Here is a short list of core assumptions, principles, and basic ideas nurtured by our history and its morality around which most academics still organize their lives. Notice as they are given that these values appear as matched pairs, yet, each cluster is accompanied by a rider—that is, by a word that represents a consequence of the two words standing for the ideas of value.

Diversity and pluralism, leading to its concomitant, relativism, are foundation stones for the American House of Intellect. We speak of the diversity in types of institutions—1,200 community colleges, 700 church-related colleges, 3,200 four-year institutions. We applaud the demographic diversity in our communities—racial minorities, older students. Then there are the alternative delivery systems—corporate classrooms, degree programs at military bases, study centers in retirement communities. Diversity in structures and functions is accompanied by pluralism in educational philosophy and instructional methodology. The expanding diversity and resultant pluralism of higher education in this country are seen not only as its most conspicuous features but as its most distinguishing characteristics. These are basic ideas that are highly valued.

There are, however, noticeable shadows cast by these shining values. Diversity and pluralism have been carried so far as to embrace contradiction. The flip comment of faculty members conceals yet reveals their unease at this state of affairs—"The only things we have in common are our differences. We agree to disagree." Consequently, the institution once characterized by its unity is now likely to be characterized by its divisions.

The resulting separation, isolation, and even fragmentation do not exhaust the consequence of this condition. Diversity and pluralism carry with them that corollary already mentioned—moral relativism. In his big book, *Modern Times,* Paul Johnson says that modern times began when Einstein's theory of relativity was finally confirmed (1919).[10] Rarely if ever has such an abstract scientific theory so captured the public imagination. Only a few people were able to understand it as a theory of physics, but there were vast numbers ready to refine relativity as relativism and to apply it to morals, religion, politics, and all bourgeois values. Clearly, the materials for a social revolution were at hand.

Johnson observes that the subsequent decline and, ultimately, the collapse of the religious impulse in much of the West would leave a huge vacuum. And the record of modern times is the record of how that vacuum has been filled. If God is no longer the basis of authority, nor the Bible, who or what will meet the need? Nietzsche gave the answer—the "will to power." And in Lenin, Hitler, Mao, and scores of other tyrants of the twentieth century, we see what happens when the vacuum is filled by persons who impose order without feeling any obligation to ethics and who have only one idea about virtue—that virtue is a vice.[11]

With the historical record making clear that we cannot live in a world devoid of tradition and authority, now as before, the battle is on to decide which type of authority and which interpretation of tradition will prevail. This means that in the modern university we need to make clear that a commitment to substantive diversity does not mean a commitment to undifferentiated pluralism, to pluralism carried to the point of contradiction. We must work together to determine appropriate limits to pluralism. And those limits will not be set, I believe, by resorting to the lowest common denominator, as relativism would have it. That course of action leads on into emotivism and subjectivism. That's bad enough, but the tragedy is compounded when the danger of chaos is brought up short by imposed order, by order rigidly enforced by tyrannical authority.

That word "authority" opens the door for us to see a second linked pair of ideas, ideas of value that still guide colleges and universities—even in this time of considerable ideational disarray.

If academics cannot any longer accept a unifying authority outside themselves, if they cannot submit to the sovereignty of God, or to the power of the nation-state, or to some variation of natural law, then they make the basis for authority the solitary individual or a collection of like-minded individuals. And if academics cannot serve concepts such as justice, truth, and beauty—because there are only contingent truths, and beauty is in the eye of the beholder, and justice is an evolving concept determined more by life than logic (as Oliver Wendell Holmes once said)—then they turn toward something more accessible and more easily understood by the individual and by colleagues; they turn toward their own resources, especially their own subject-matter specializations and the cognate competencies. Indeed, those words are linked words that have become ideas of values—specialization and competency, leading to professionalism.

Here is the way Professor Sheldon Rothblatt of the University of California, Berkeley, describes the situation confronting scholars and scientists:

> Today we have gone so far beyond a world of final causes that even the search for truth has an uncomfortable dimension. The extra-ordinary explosion of information and proliferation of modes of thinking have made it impossible for any one mind to comprehend but a small portion of what is known. In despair the intellect turns back upon itself, creating its own world of rules and looking for reassurance in heuristic models which it is tempted to substitute for reality.[12]

The modern faculty member, in most institutions of higher education, gives his or her primary loyalty not to the colleges or university within which the work is carried forward. It is, rather, within the professional association or guild that the work is defined and quality-control standards are set. It is to the "community of competence" that faculty feels mainly accountable.

There is a positive or sunny side to this. Academic professionals are dignified by the fact that, if truly professional, they provide an essential service to society; a service requiring skills not easily acquired, indeed, secured only over a considerable period of time and at considerable expense; a basic service with a set of skills having a serious body of scholarship and research, knowledge, and information behind them. And all of this—the service and the skills, the facts and their applications—are to be used carefully, for the betterment of society. No wonder that the professoriat at its best is viewed with respect, even awe.

But again, there is a shadow side. The rider word to specialization and competence is professionalism. To be sure, it can convey ideas of great value. On the other hand, the professionalization of the professoriat has meant, too often, that professionalism is defined only as technical specialization—skill spared the responsibility of moral judgment. And competency is no longer accountable to the general public or even to the constituency of the college or university but, instead, is accountable only to the closed order of peers or to that community of competence.

There is another consequence, another danger. In the name of professionalism, faculty and administrators too may insist on extensive personal freedom, usually in the name of "academic freedom." And they will push for the spirit of independence and individuality in expression, unfettered by the countervailing claims of community with its emphasis on collective judgment and shared responsibility. When this happens, these faculty or administrators become the enemies of efforts to keep individuality and community in balance. The college of consequence is a place where personal freedom and one's individuality are both encouraged so long as equal attention is given to collective judgments, to our human interdependency, and to the claims of community.

The preceding sets of deep principles or basic values are examples of what has here been called ideas of value. As shown, they carry tension within themselves and provide correctives to each other. But, finally they can and must go forward together if we are to reconcile history and morality.

It is the terrible tension between unvarnished history and undiluted morality that makes an effective reconciliation so difficult in a university community. There are elements of Western history that are simply unworthy to be honored. The status of women and of racial minorities call out for change, not continuity. Yet, we know from history that change that breaks too harshly from tradition, moving away too abruptly, endangers the change more than the tradition. And as for morality, its authority has often been twisted into authoritarianism, where titles replace skills or age stands in for competence. In true morality, character and compassion go everywhere together. But when morality is distorted, interdiction is prized over remission, "thus far and no farther" over "even so." Nevertheless, given the complexities of both history and morality, even dialogue is difficult and reconciliation seems always to be partial and imperfect. Perhaps the best we can hope for is that the university worthy of the name will show by its actions that it is responding to the challenge raised by Octavio Paz, the challenge to reconcile history and morality. The university at its best knows that true authority, essential to its usefulness, cannot be separated from its history. Nor will the university's claim to integrity be respected if what the institution does cannot be shown to be a moral endeavor.

In one of Robertson Davies's essays, this great Canadian novelist makes the point on which to conclude.

> The world is full of people who think they could write or who have, at some time, written. But they do not stay with it. Why? Is it because the real writer, the serious writer, who is a writer all his life, is a special kind of person? Yes, it is. And what kind of person is he? I do not pretend to be able to answer the question fully, for there are many kinds of writers. But they all have a characteristic, indeed a distinguishing trait in their psychological make-up, that makes them recognizable, and I call it the writer's conscience. I use the phrase to describe the continuing struggle that goes on in the psyche of any writer of importance. And by that expression "any writer of importance" I exclude the journalistic word-spinners, the ghost writers, the concocters of literary confectionary, although

some of them are remarkable technicians. I am talking about the writer who tries—perhaps not all the time but certainly throughout the better part of his career—to write the best that he can about the themes that concern him most.[13]

Davies's point about writers can be applied to educators and even to the educational institutions within which they work. There is not only a writer's conscience, but there is also an educator's conscience and, beyond that, a college conscience. In addition, there is, or should be, a continuing struggle that goes on not only in the writer of importance but in the university of importance. It is precisely this struggle with the most consequential issues—individuality and community, change and tradition—that separates the true educator and the university of quality from the collegiate equivalent of the journalistic word-spinners, the ghost writers, and the concocters of literary confectionary. The quality of the struggle will be shown as the university and its leaders grapple with this difficult but essential task of reconciling morality and history. When you see educators struggling with issues of that magnitude, you will know that you are witnessing a struggle worth the struggle.

Notes

1. Octavio Paz, *One Earth, Four or Five Worlds: Reflection on Contemporary History,* trans. Helen R. Lane (San Diego: Harcourt Brace Janovich, 1985), 49.

2. Albert E. Elson, "What Isn't Modern Sculpture?" *ARTnews* 86 (Jan. 1987): 145.

3. Robert Hughes, "The Liberty of Thought Itself," *Time,* Sept. 1, 1986, p. 86.

4. Hannah Arendt, *Between Past and Future: Eight Exercises in Political Thought* (New York: Viking, 1968), 195.

5. Steven Muller, "At 350, the U.S. University Is Vast but Unfocused," *New York Times,* Sept. 7, 1986, p. 14.

6. Gerald Grant, "The Character of Education and the Education of Character," *Kettering Review* (Fall 1985): 30.

7. Elson, "What Isn't Modern Sculpture?" 147.

8. John Gardner, "The Moral Aspect of Leadership," *Leadership Papers/5,* fifth in a series of papers prepared for the Leadership Studies Program sponsored by Independent Sector, a nonprofit coalition of 600 organizations (1987): 14–15.

9. Ibid., 15.

10. Paul Johnson, *Modern Times: The World From the Twenties to the Eighties* (New York: Harper and Row, 1983), 4–5.

11. Alasdair C. MacIntyre, "The Nature of Moral Disagreement Today and the Claims of Emotivism," in *After Virtue: A Study in Moral Theory* (Notre Dame, Ind.: University of Notre Dame Press, 1981), 6–21.

12. Sheldon Rothblatt, *Tradition and Change,* in *English Liberal Education* (London: Faber and Faber, 1976), 197.

13. Robertson Davies, "The Conscience of the Writer," in his book *One Half of Robertson Davies* (New York: Viking, 1978), 121–22.

CAN THE HUMANITIES STILL HUMANIZE HIGHER EDUCATION?

8

James T. Laney

THE DECADE OF THE EIGHTIES has been a decade of judgment for American education, from the 1981 report of the National Commission on Excellence in Education, *A Nation at Risk*, to the 1987 best-seller by Allan Bloom, *The Closing of the American Mind*. Perhaps no judgment sounded more strident than that of former Secretary of Education William Bennett, who accused higher education of being rich and wanting to get richer, of charging too much tuition, and, most devastatingly, of not doing a good job. In this last accusation, he was echoing Ernest L. Boyer's 1981 Carnegie report, *A Quest for Common Learning*, which bemoaned the loss of the core curriculum and, along with it, the glories of our heritage and our sense of tradition and civility. Of course none of us in higher education likes to be criticized, so many of us pointed to increased costs and dismissed Secretary Bennett's position as simplistic.

Now, however, without presuming to speak for higher education but only for myself, I must acknowledge that there is something very important in Mr. Bennett's remarks. The fact is that he was simply saying in public what a lot of people have been saying in private. There is a growing public uneasiness with higher education, a grow-

James T. Laney is president of Emory University, Atlanta, Georgia.

ing resistance to its cost, a general disenchantment. The public no longer believes uncritically in education. The system continues to work, after a fashion, but that is because the ultimate stakes are high. The universities do, after all, give credentials, and those credentials are worth a lot today, at least in the marketplace.

It is true that some institutions seem to be moving in the direction recommended by the Boyer report. MIT, for example, has reordered its curriculum to correct an imbalance between the technical courses in which it so excels and the humanities and liberal arts. MIT apparently wants its students to graduate with some perspective on the ends and consequences of technology as well as with the ability to use it. So far, so good. Recently, however, the faculty have revealed the real reason for this new curriculum: they are tired of MIT graduates working for Yale graduates! They want their alumni, who they rightly feel are as good as any, to run the businesses and not simply be the scientists and engineers who work for others.

MIT's example, initially promising, turns out to be symptomatic of the careerist emphasis in our universities today. Careerism rules our institutions, and there is a corresponding narrowing of interest in and concern for the larger world. I feel very strongly that we must give our students more humanities, more liberal arts — or at least what they represent — if we are to provide them with a real education and not just with sophisticated training. But I'm not at all sure that yet another reordering of course requirements will accomplish the ends I have in mind. In most of our institutions, the issue is not really one of curriculum balance; it is one of *ethos,* the spirit or tone of the whole university. The very ethos of the humanities has largely disappeared from most of our campuses. It has been eroded even within the liberal arts themselves, many of which have come to concentrate on technique and methodology, much like the sciences which, unfortunately, they seek to ape.

One of the things we do not do well enough or often enough in higher education is to identify just what it is that the humanities and the liberal arts traditionally have stood for. What is that? What is the world that they create and portray? Literature, art, history, philosophy, and religion set forth the resonant world of human experience in all its complexity, the world of human struggle and aspiration and tragedy, where life itself is shaped and given voice and direction. This is the world where chaos, in thought or act, becomes ordered and civilized, where students begin to catch a glimpse of something larger or grander than themselves, even while they continue to wrestle with the demons within them. This is the larger world revealed by the arts and humanities, a transmutation of the narrower everyday world whose urgent demands and whose pressure to be self-contained, if not self-absorbed, exert a powerful and seductive influence on both our students and ourselves.

In short, the humanities are concerned with humanizing, with transforming the elf and the animal within us all. The goal of classical education was to draw students out of themselves into a larger and more worthy vision of life and the good society in all its wholeness and integrity. Young and old alike shared the quest for that larger world, and this sharing was the hallmark of great teaching. I believe that most of us who have chosen to go into higher education were inspired to do so because at some point we were touched by a great teacher. It was not a matter of technique or methodology or mastery, although those may have dazzled us, but a glimpse of a life which, in its honesty—not in its perfection, but in its honesty and integrity and discipline—was inspiring and alluring. We wanted to participate in such a life.

So it was that, embodied in great teachers, the humanities gave rise to an ethos which subtly shaped, oriented, and made alert and sensible—in short, *educated*—the minds and spirits of a younger generation. It did not, at least at its best, indoctrinate or proselytize or forestall discussion and debate. It suggested the height and breadth to which a full life might aspire. It provided the tools for critical judgment—of people, events, institutions, and societies—and for the puncturing of illusion, hypocrisy, pomposity, and self-seeking.

This ethos which at one time suffused the curriculum, and indeed the campus, has largely disappeared. It has been replaced by another ethos far more pragmatic and utilitarian. I don't know how to characterize it except by the barbaric word "professionalization." We don't educate students today so much as "professionalize" them, giving them the tools of mastery and the credentials for entry into the world of work but no longer introducing them to the larger world of wisdom. We simply give them a toolbox and pack them off.

How did this occur, this substitution of the one ethos for the other? I think there was a conjunction, a complicity, of two factors. On the one hand, our incoming students were increasingly driven by an impatience for credentialing, a desire to get on with it, an orientation toward success. On the other hand, there arose within the university a host of disciplines and specialties that no longer tried to comprehend anything like a whole picture or a larger ethos. What began as a laudatory tendency, a move toward higher standards and more rigorous procedures, has ended up entangling the academy in a web of tightly focused disciplines, perfected methodology, and increasingly structured mastery creating ever more elegant and isolated systems of thought and discourse. Driven by the tenure system, by careerism, by intellectual politics, by publication, the faculty find themselves under enormous pressure to concentrate on these self-reflexive modes. As a result, they no longer feel competent to take a wider view, nor do they have the time for it. Few professors have the latitude, the breathing space, to explore the larger questions and concerns. Few students have the leisure so essential to risk-taking and productive thought, the time to spend in learning that doesn't have to pay off in a grade-point average that will get one into law school or medical school.

At the same time that the direction of higher education has become increasingly careerist, the outside guilds and professional organizations have been exerting increasing control over the university curriculum. Coming to a focus on the campus, the demands of the various guilds virtually drive the academic disciplines. Whether these disciplines fit together in any coherent pattern or even a useful constellation of skills is purely a matter of chance. So the ethos of the university has come to be dominated by the professional, the specialist, without adequate attention to the large picture, to wholeness, to integrity. This professionalization of the curriculum fosters a manipulative cynicism among our students, an emphasis on the quick payoff and the bottom line.

We see this in medicine, for example. The *Journal of the American*

Medical Association has carried articles decrying the increasing cynicism of medical students, their declining humanity, their overtly mercenary attitudes, even their dishonesty. We see it in law, where the number of Yale Law School graduates entering public service has declined 75 percent in fifteen years. At Columbia it is down even more. Many students express impatience with more reflective courses and refuse to do pro bono work. Not long ago I asked a prominent attorney how his firm handled pro bono cases. It was an innocent question, but he was embarrassed. "We don't handle them," he said. "When I started with the firm, each of us had to spend so many hours a week doing pro bono work. That was the way it was. But at some point in the last ten years, there was a rebellion. So now the firm simply hires lawyers to do our pro bono work for us, while the junior partners spend all their time working furiously to make partner, with the clock running. The clock doesn't run when you're working pro bono."

Needless to say, we also see this same spirit among the MBAs, even to the extent that some top executives have come to view the attitudes of business school graduates with a somewhat jaundiced eye. John Scully, the chairman of Apple, once said he would not hire business majors or MBA graduates; he wants liberal arts majors who have some judgment of people, of events, of institutions and society, who can put something together. Unfortunately, such graduates are harder and harder to find these days, even among liberal arts majors. The students, the faculty, the guilds—all of them are pressing for the quick payoff, the bottom line. This combination of pressures is *deforming* education, and it is deforming the professions as well.

What observations could one make in the light of this situation? First of all, the faculty cannot expect students to do or to attend to what they themselves do not attend to. Despite their demurrals, the faculty *are* role models. Their modesty says, "Oh no, we're not." What they really are saying is self-protective: "We don't want to be role models; that's too heavy." But the fact is that no matter how high you go in learning—to the Ph.D. or the chief residency in medical school—students follow their mentors with such attentiveness that they are bound to be shaped by that relationship. The transactions between student and professor are powerful and complex. They are not simply limited to the skill at hand; they comprehend a whole way of living and looking at life. And if there is honor, if there is restraint, if there is worthiness, these will be communicated.

Secondly, I do not think we can expect the faculty to do or to attend to what the university itself does not value. Our universities have become great engines of entrepreneurship. They are not simply multiversities; they are conglomerates with a powerful institutional initiative. At its best, that initiative is good; it moves ahead. But there is also a darker side; there is the competitive bidding for faculty, even the competitive *building* for research grants. We build new facilities, and we bid against each other for faculty stars—not just individuals but whole teams of people. We build great departments like football teams. We are not adding to the sum total of knowledge or good; we are just moving the players from here to there, and the price goes up accordingly.

I realize, of course, that today's university is expected to do many things—research, the dissemination of knowledge, service—and that these things take big money and people of enormous ability. But where do the students fit into this high-powered operation? There is a terrific condescension involved when we start to talk about the big-time activities of the university. The president and vice presidents and deans are running around dealing with important things; the people who used to teach, if they are really good, are off dealing with important things—their research or their consultancies or their television appearances. Faced with this big-time operation, where everybody is busy doing important things, it is very hard for the students not to feel that they are in a sort of side show. But maybe we should reconsider our priorities. We are talking about the next generation of leaders. We are talking about the people who are going to take our place. We are talking about their quality of life and their vision of society. What could be more important than this?

There is a tension here that goes right down into the heart of the university. The professional and entrepreneurial involvements I have mentioned are of great value to the institution as well as to the prospective members of the guilds. No university can rise to eminence without participating in them. But there is, I believe, a negative correlation between these involvements and the university's commitment to the arts and humanities. Once the element of power is introduced into the world of thought, there is an inevitable corruption. I do not say that power has no right to exist; but I think that the larger ethos I have been referring to requires something of a withdrawal from the world of affairs.

What can we do to counter this deforming of higher education? First of all, we need to begin by redefining the fundamental idea of a university. We have not done that in a long time; Clark Kerr's rather tired characterization is long overdue for revision. The university is not simply a neutral playing field, nor is it simply a multifaceted conglomerate. We need to set some internal priorities, and we need to define our relation to society on our own terms rather than simply taking on society's agenda without any critical consideration.

Clearly, the faculty is going to have to be involved in this enterprise. That will be a time-consuming process; I have no illusions about what is involved in undertaking such a task in a pluralistic university. One step we have taken at Emory is to organize a series of interdisciplinary faculty seminars with the aim of developing a common language across the various disciplines and fields. I am also hopeful that these seminars will engender a greater critical spirit within the university. The fact is that on the whole we are far too docile; there needs to be a lot more skepticism. I do not mean destructive cynicism: I mean that we need to do a lot more hard thinking about the most fundamental assumptions and axioms and postulates that are operating in our culture, our time, our world. The university is not providing that hard thinking. Too much is strategic; too much is tactical; too much is oriented toward what will work and what is prudential and utilitarian.

Another way of countering this bottom-line mentality is to relax some of the more destructive aspects of the tenure system and careerist pressures generally. I do not think we will get less quality. The fact is that the present system is forcing our younger faculty to go right down the middle of their discipline, where there is little risk, where it is very safe, where they will do the job. But that is not where any real contribution and creativity are going to come from. The real breakthroughs almost always occur in the margins of a discipline where it overlaps with other fields. It is an interesting fact that most of our departments and disciplines were defined and established around 1900. There have been many new developments since then. We should not assume that the shape and scope of these disciplines are laid down in stone.

Another thing the universities need to do is to take a far more aggressive position on the question of professional standards, especially in law and medicine. The legal and medical professions represent a sector of society that is neither public nor private, a sphere that traditionally has been ordered and governed by a sense of institutionalized honor and restraint. That restraint is largely gone, and now it is full speed ahead. We have almost reached the point where the idea of ethics comes down to what is illegal, what you can prove in court. In the face of this decline, it is up to the universities to reintroduce the notion of professional honor and self-restraint. The professions must stop lionizing the greedy. We need to resurrect the concepts of approbation and disapprobation. Some things are more worthy than others, and some things are downright despicable. These ought to be pointed out, and the university must participate in attempting that.

Finally, I think we have to provide the students with greater access to the faculty. One place to begin is a program of freshman seminars, meeting once a week in little groups with the same faculty member, all of them having the same reading agenda, so that everyone in the freshman class is reading something in common. This would not be terribly burdensome, but it could mean a great deal. The faculty should also have opportunities to meet with larger groups of students in town-hall-type sessions, something like "The Last Lecture Series" where professors respond to the question, If you had only one more hour to speak, what would you say? Such a framework can help faculty to see their own discipline in a larger perspective, and it can give them a legitimate reason to share some of the things that are most important to them.

What *is* most important? As I think about this, it occurs to me that the universities' response to the South African situation provides a litmus test both for ourselves and for our students—not what the response of a university has been, but how that response was arrived at. Does the university have a thinking, moral center? Is there any place within the university from which we can offer a response greater than a prudential response? Where does that center locate itself, the moral center of the university? That is the crucial question, and, until we can answer it, we are not fulfilling our highest function: to embody and articulate for our students and ourselves the larger world of truth, and goodness, and civilization, which is our heritage and our legacy to future generations.

MORAL VALUES AND
HIGHER EDUCATION

9

Jeffrey R. Holland

THE ISSUES OF values and morality and citizenship and character development in higher education, however elusive and ill-defined—or differently defined—those words may be, have been my principal preoccupation for the nine years I have served as a university president. Although I do not wish to turn back the higher education clock to some convenient hour in the nineteenth century (or earlier!), I do think that we might need to relearn some of the lessons taught by our forebears about what James T. Laney alludes to as "the education of the heart." He writes:

> Until a few decades ago . . . education was seen as a moral endeavor, not because it sought to indoctrinate but because it was a sharing of things that people held to be important. . . .
> . . . Education was the institutionalization of what we as a people deemed to be important. . . .
> But times have changed. . . .
> . . . [W]hat we are emphasizing today, largely by default, is careerism. We seem to be turning out people who are bent upon

Jeffrey R. Holland is past president of Brigham Young University and is currently a member of the First Quorum of Seventy of The Church of Jesus Christ of Latter-day Saints.

exploiting careers for their own ends rather than upon service through their professions for the sake of society.

And that is exactly what we are bound to do if we do not educate the heart.[1]

Obviously there is much to do merely in getting better reading and writing and mathematical performance from our students. Professor Sandalow makes the persuasive case in his essay that "the university's greatest potential for influencing the moral development of students is in the contribution that it can make to their intellectual development." But in a world now consumed by discussions about taxes, I wish to apply the "value added" question to university life. If every university, through some yet-to-be-legislated tax, were to get financial compensation for the "value added" to its graduates in 1988, what would be the "value(s)" and how much would be "added"? Do students walk away from a university in the last quarter of the twentieth century with *moral* evidence that they have been there, moral evidence that would have been assumed and expected in any academic century but our own?

I was invited to speak in Washington on this subject in 1984, and the issues seem to me to have become more important, not less, as time passes. In our respective states and nations the economic plight of schools both public and private is being hotly debated and feverishly reviewed. We are awash in a flood of reports and studies. In the United States we have recently seen higher education examined by the Carnegie Foundation, which says that "the undergraduate college, the very heart of higher learning, is a troubled institution";[2] the National Endowment for the Humanities has asked us to "reclaim a legacy"[3] which seems to some nearly lost; a host of task forces are insisting on "action for excellence";[4] and recently Secretary Bennett has repeated his assertion that most students in colleges and universities are not getting what they pay for. And, of course, these are only evidences of national anguish; a gaggle of state and local reports have pursued the same agenda closer to our respective homes. Business barons, social scientists, public policymakers, and skeptical taxpayers are wading into the swamp to grapple with educational reform each in his or her own way.

Not all of the reports are limited to higher education nor do they make the same recommendations, but one of the earliest and most publicized, a report submitted to then-Secretary T. H. Bell by the National Commission on Excellence in Education, is representative. Its title is in its opening line.

> Our Nation is at risk. Our once unchallenged preeminence in commerce, industry, science, and technological innovation is being overtaken by competitors throughout the world. . . . The educational foundations of our society are presently being eroded by a rising tide of mediocrity that threatens our very future as a Nation and as a people. What was unimaginable a generation ago has begun to occur—others are matching and surpassing our education attainments.
>
> If an unfriendly foreign power had attempted to impose on America the mediocre educational performance that exists today, we might well have viewed it as an act of war. . . . We have, in effect, been committing an act of unthinking, unilateral educational disarmament.
>
> Our society and its educational institutions seem to have lost sight of the basic purposes of schooling, and of the high expectations and disciplined effort needed to attain them.[5]

Then to demonstrate that the "basic purposes of schooling" have indeed been lost, the commission reports that the Japanese make better automobiles than we do, the South Koreans make better steel mills than we do, the Germans make finer machine tools than we do, and so forth. Thus we are told, our nation is at risk.

My concern after three or four years of reading such reports and listening to them being endlessly discussed is that, while a *nation* may be at risk, it is manifestly clear that a very important American *notion* is at even greater risk.

As evidenced by their frequent and conspicuous absence from *most* of these reports and proposals—not all, but certainly the early ones— we have obviously relegated all the moral and civic (read "civilizing") values of education to the back of the bus—if indeed they are still being allowed to ride at all—while prominently seated up front are the real necessities, those which gave primacy to our economic needs, our escalating technological needs; in short those that are "unabashedly utilitarian." As Professor Douglas Sloan has said, "First a living, then art and morality; first survival for our financially beleaguered colleges and universities, and only then a philosophy of higher education."[6] And university presidents—my colleagues and I—are conspicuously among the guilty. A university president recently said, "I really believe there has got to be a resurgence of public commitment to education in this country, and I think it's fundamental if we really do want to see economic growth, advancement in national defense, and an increase in productivity. . . . This has got to become the nation's number one priority."[7]

If our number one priority in this or any country is education devoted to economic growth, national defense, and increased productivity, important as they are, then I believe God in his heaven cannot help us reclaim any university legacy. No wonder Amitai Etzioni speaks of the 1980s as "the hollowing of America."[8] Meg Greenfield saw the wrongheadedness of it all when she wrote several months ago that

> the values we bring to the effort to right the situation are precisely the ones that got us in trouble in the first place and are only likely to perpetuate our grief.
>
> Education as an "investment," education as a way to beat the Russians, and best the Japanese, education as a way to get ahead of the fellow down the street . . . you really do not generate the educational values that count when you stress only these external, comparative advantages.[9]

In the words of Robert Nash and Edward Ducharme, "[The report's] deficiencies are a direct outgrowth of what is essentially a manpower-needs view of educational excellence, a view which encourages a marketplace solution to complex spiritual and intellectual problems."[10]

What is missing, they say, is "the most irksome (yet the most important) question of all: what should education's short- and long-term purposes be *beyond* [a] response to . . . manpower needs."[11]

It is, it seems to me, as if Leo Strauss's classic *Natural Right and History* speaks directly to our hour. "We can be . . . wise in all matters of secondary importance, but we have to be resigned to utter ignorance in the most important respect. . . . We are then in the position of beings who are sane and sober when engaged in trivial business and who gamble like madmen when confronted with serious issues—[it is] retail sanity and wholesale madness."[12]

James Reston made something of this same point in a *New York Times* article about political leadership. "It's interesting to look back," he says, "at the speeches and the Federalist Papers at the beginning of the American Republic. Their authors were tough politicians, but they were always referring to their responsibilities to 'future generations.' The talk here in modern times is mainly about the next election."[13]

Then, quoting Walter Lippmann, Reston goes on. "Those in high places . . . are more than the administrators of government bureaus. They are more than the writers of laws. They are the custodians of a nation's ideals, of the beliefs it cherishes, of the faith which makes a nation out of a mere aggregation of individuals."[14]

"Leaders do matter," he concludes. "Much depends on how they view themselves, what they say, whether they appeal to the best or the worst in the people."[15] If that kind of leadership matters in politics, then surely it must matter in education. Professors and presidents are in "high places." They are—or should most assuredly be—"custodians of a nation's ideals, of the beliefs it cherishes, of the faith which makes a nation out of a mere aggregation of individuals." That is, after all, why all those young Athenians went to Socrates in the first place. Educational leaders "do matter" and as a profession we need to appeal to "the best in the people." The nation may be educationally at risk, all right, but not solely for the reasons expressed by the National Commission—indeed, not even principally for the reasons they express. As a nation we have lost sight of "the basic purposes of schooling" [to use their phrase] but so, it seems to me, have far too many of our own colleagues. Where are the Thoreauvian men and women who will strike at the root of our educational— and national—problems rather than hacking forever at the branches? Too many in our profession have forgotten what Socrates said in those original and purer groves of academe—"for the argument," he said to his students, "is not about just any question but about the way one should live."[16] Losing the significant sense of that notion has put our nation at risk. It is the greater crisis in American education, for there is the real "rising tide of mediocrity."

We know that at least Socrates' very best student tried to address the teacher's question. Against the Sophists, those itinerant charlatans who said they could teach fifth-century B.C. Athenians how to be clever and win debates so long as they didn't worry about "the truth" (of which, relatively speaking, they felt certain there wasn't any), Plato held that not only was there truth but that the highest truth always had moral value. To know it and live according to it was a man's obligation and his virtue. Finally, for him, only education in virtue was worthy of the name. Plato's philosophy provided a justification not only for what students ought to be taught but for how they ought to live.

That philosophy provided what Alston Chase calls "the paradigmatic rationale for scholarly activity"[17] from the fifth century B.C. to the nineteenth century A.D.

Even during the very darkest moments in our history it endured. St. Benedict, living at a time when Rome was threatened and finally overrun by Vandals, simply retreated behind the stone walls of Monte Cassino, taking with him the spirit and his valued traditions in Christianity. "While the barbarian invaders ran wild," notes Calvin Woodard, "pillaging and destroying everything in sight, St. Benedict and his monks gently nurtured the flickering flame of civilization."[18]

St. Benedict's example reminds us that one of the purposes of education is not only to resist the wicked, the tawdry, and the profane, but to stand unalterably for the higher values of civilization—Plato's truths, if you will—and, when the turbulent world will not accept them, to preserve and keep them alive for the future—when and after the Vandals have exhausted themselves.

And so it continued, out of the darkness and into the light. "Learning and training in virtue are peculiar to man," they would still write in the fifteenth century. "We call those studies liberal that are worthy of a free man; those studies by which we obtained and practice virtue and wisdom; that education which calls forth, trains, and develops those highest gifts of body and mind, which ennoble men and are rightly judged to rank next in dignity to virtue only."[19]

From continental and English Renaissance to the shore of the

New World, the universities were charged with molding the moral character of their students.

In the new United States such personal beliefs as John Adams's virtuous citizen[20] and Thomas Jefferson's moral sense and "aristocracy of talent and virtue"[21] were the natural values upon which the Republic was predicated. Jefferson always placed the individual man first in his philosophy and framed his entire social theory in the light of the moral nature of that human being.

The key to John Adams's optimism was his abiding belief in American virtue. Even during the darkest hours of the Revolution, he felt "the great difficulties which America faced, would 'lay the Foundations of a full and flourishing People, deep and strong in great Virtues and abilities.' "[22] He believed firmly that history (under the direction of divine providence) was the story of man's search for liberty and that America was destined to become the next and greatest in the continuing succession of empires—a land where the two great bulwarks of liberty and knowledge would flourish. But none of this meant that virtue was either automatic or inevitable. It required education and discipline. The Founding Fathers had read John Locke with a passion and they believed with him that "of all the Men we meet with, Nine Parts of Ten are what they are, Good or Evil, useful or not, by their Education."[23] The great danger to society, then, was not from any innate evil within the individual, but rather from ignorance born of sloth. Laziness, both moral and intellectual, was at the heart of the problem.

That is why Benjamin Franklin believed that an individual, in devoting himself to his own intellectual and moral development in a disciplined way, not only insures his success in life but also determines his society's moral progress. "Virtue is an art," Franklin maintained, "as much as painting, architecture, or navigation. If a person wants to become a painter, a navigator, or an architect . . . one must learn 'the Principles of the Art.' "[24] Even the pessimistic James Madison said, "I go on this great republican principle, that the people will have virtue and intelligence to select men of virtue and wisdom. Is there no virtue among us? If there be not, we are in a wretched situation. . . . To suppose that any form of government will secure liberty or happiness without any virtue in the people, is a chimerical idea."[25] As Professor Douglas Sloan has so carefully documented, the moral foundation for the Republic both informed and encouraged the same foundation for the American educational experience. Until the very last decade of the nineteenth century, the most important course in the college curriculum was moral philosophy, taught usually by the college president and required of all senior students. It aimed to integrate, to give meaning and purpose to the student's entire college experience and course of study. In so doing it more importantly sought to equip the graduating seniors with the ethical sensitivity and insight needed if they were to put their newly acquired knowledge to use in ways that would benefit not only themselves and their own personal advancement, but the larger society as well.

So the foremost task of the moral philosopher was to demonstrate to his students that humans are fundamentally moral creatures. It was his task to exhort, admonish, and inspire students to recognize that the demands of morality were real and all-encompassing. Furthermore, the entire college curriculum and campus environment had the same purpose. The entire college experience was meant above all to be an experience in character development and the moral life.

But the advent of the twentieth century brought decisive change, including the rise of the modern university. Yet Daniel Coit Gilman, president of Johns Hopkins, the new model of the research university, still spoke for most of his fellow university reformers when he said, "The object of the university is to develop character—to make men."[26] But there was change in the wind.

Diversity and specialization, trained experts, the rise of scholarly societies, the elective principle introduced under Charles W. Eliot at Harvard, the growth of university departments, undergraduate specialization, vocationalism, professional education, and research— all of these shattered the vision of a unified curriculum and culture of learning. The ethical, social, and character concerns once central to higher education were giving way to an emphasis on research and specialized training as the primary purpose of the university.

With the new status and scholarly achievements of the faculties came an academic style that was becoming, in the words of Frederick Rudolph, "indifferent to undergraduates," "removed from moral judgment," and to an increasing degree "unrelated to the traditional social purposes of higher education."[27]

There was increasing emphasis on "value-free inquiry"—and for good reason. By dispensing with such ethical questions, the scholars also eliminated a major source of potential controversy. The teaching of ethics was relegated to the department of philosophy—where there was little danger that anyone would enroll in it. The classic texts by America's nineteenth-century moral philosophers had been almost totally abandoned. "With the world calling for moral power and efficiency, and with the adolescent of college years in the nascent period of moral adjustment," wrote one early student of the teaching of ethics, "how insufficient, foreign, barbarian, do the arid ethical logomachies of most textbooks appear?"[28]

Some, sensing the loss, tried anxiously to reclaim their cultural and, indeed, religious heritage. The general education movement in the first half of the twentieth century consisted largely of experiments whose "central concern was moral education, the turning out of persons with the breadth of knowledge, intellectual discipline, and ethical sensitivity needed to grapple with the personal and social problems of the modern world."[29]

One of the earliest efforts was made at Columbia in 1917. Concerning that effort, Harry Carman commented that those charged with looking into the problem agreed that the college "should be concerned with education for effective citizenship in a democratic society [—with producing] citizens with broad perspective and a critical and constructive approach to life, who are concerned about values in terms of integrity of character, motives, attitudes, and excellence of behavior; citizens who have the ability to think, to communicate, to make intelligent and wise judgments, to evaluate moral situations, and to work effectively to good ends with others."[30]

Twenty-five years later, following the lead of Robert Hutchins at Chicago, President James Conant of Harvard appointed a committee to study "the objectives for general education in a free society." In their report the committee pointed out that "the impulse to rear students to a received idea of the good is in fact necessary to education. It is impossible to escape the realization that our society, like any society, rests on common beliefs and that a major task of education is to perpetuate them."

But it was hard work and we seemed to be failing. As Walter Lippmann wrote at the time,

> We reject the religious and classical heritage, first, because to master it requires more effort than we are willing to compel ourselves to make and, second, because it creates issues that are too deep and too contentious to be faced with equanimity. We have abolished the old curriculum because we are afraid of it, afraid to face any longer in a modern democratic society the severe discipline and the deep, disconcerting issues of the nature of the universe, and of man's place in it and of his destiny.[32]

Then came the "effortless barbarism" of the third quarter of this century, my own years at Yale, when grand educational institutions — and more than a few grand educators — were savaged by the very students who had come to those centers to be civilized. The late sixties and early seventies were the darkest hours in the history of American higher education, a dark night of the institutional soul from which we have not yet recovered — and may never fully recover. In their disdain for standards and the demand for relevance, our cultural continuity was eroded and any institutional sense of morality regarding a student's course work, conversation, conduct, or sexual activity was obliterated. Our Benedictine walls around campus were not thick enough in those years, and perhaps neither were our convictions.

Now, we are taking another look at the inseparability of living and learning. If we are not diligent, it may be as Montaigne wrote: "They teach us to live, when life is past. A hundred students have caught the syphilis before they came to Aristotle's lesson on temperance."[33]

Surely some criticism from our present plight has to be directed toward me and my fellow presidents, who should have been in the forefront all these years, "custodians of the nation's ideals,"[34] declaring the difference between right and wrong.

Consider this story told to me by Alston Chase. A friend of his was teaching at a small liberal arts college. One of his students vandalized her off-campus apartment in the amount of several thousand dollars, then refused to reimburse the landlord. As the college did nothing to encourage her to pay the damages, the professor took matters into his own hands. He gave her an F in the course she was taking from him and told her that he would not change it until she paid the landlord. He justified this, he told the college review board, on the solid Socratic grounds that if a student did not know right from wrong she should not pass a college course. The college authorities were incensed. The grievance committee overruled him, expunged the F from the student's record, and did not renew his contract.

The task before us is large and amorphous. The social and cultural and economic and political problems that complicate and diminish a university's moral force are challenging. But we have models to guide us. One model, Mother Teresa, when asked whether she got discouraged in the face of seemingly endless poverty, disease, and misery in the cities of India, said, "My job is not to succeed, nearly so much as it is to be faithful to my mission."[35] What is our mission? Does a university have a moral mission? Is there any sense in which that mission is moral? In what sense, if any, does the ethical and civilized future of this planet's population rest in the hands of those who teach its youth?

Notes

1. James T. Laney, "The Education of the Heart," *Harvard Magazine*, Sept.-Oct. 1985, p. 23–24.

2. "Text of Carnegie Recommendations on Undergraduate Education," *The Chronicle of Higher Education*, Nov. 5, 1986.

3. William J. Bennett, "To Reclaim a Legacy: A Report on the Humanities in Higher Education," National Endowment for the Humanities, Nov. 1984.

4. Business–Higher Education Forum, "Public Commitment to Higher Education: A Top Priority?" *Higher Education and National Affairs* 33, no. 3 (Feb. 24, 1984): 6.

5. U.S. Department of Education, National Commission on Excellence in Education, *A Nation at Risk: The Imperative for Educational Reform* (Washington, D.C.: Government Printing Office, 1983), 5–6.

6. Douglas Sloan, ed., *Education and Values* (New York: Teachers College Press, Columbia University, 1980), 1.

7. William Friday, quoted in "Public Commitment to Higher Education: A Top Priority?" 1.

8. Amitai Etzioni, *An Immodest Agenda: Rebuilding America before the Twenty-first Century* (New York: New York Press, 1983), 3.

9. Meg Greenfield, "Why Nothing is 'Wrong' Anymore," *Newsweek*, July 28, 1986, p. 72.

10. Robert J. Nash and Edward R. Ducharme, "Where There Is No Vision, the People Perish: A Nation at Risk," *Journal of Teacher Education* 34, no. 4 (July-Aug. 1983): 40.

11. Ibid.

12. Leo Strauss, *Natural Right and History* (Chicago: University of Chicago Press, 1953), 4.

13. James Reston, "Do Leaders Matter?" *The New York Times*, Aug. 31, 1983.

14. Quoted in ibid.

15. Ibid.

16. Allan Bloom, trans., *The Republic of Plato* (New York: Basic Books, 1968), 31.

17. Alston Chase, *Group Memory: A Guide to College and Student Survival in the 1980s* (Boston: Little, Brown and Company, 1980), 162–63.

18. Calvin Woodard, *The Effect of Historical Change on University Purpose* (Charlottesville: University of Virginia, Office of the Dean of Students, 1976), 7.

19. As quoted by Woodard in ibid., 15.

20. John R. Rowe, Jr., *The Changing Political Thought of John Adams* (Princeton, N.J.: Princeton University Press, 1966), 29.

21. Sloan, *Education and Values*, 194.

22. Rowe, *Changing Political Thought of John Adams*, 48–49.

23. Norman S. Fiering, "Benjamin Franklin and the Way to Virtue," *American Quarterly* 30, no 2 (Summer 1978): 210.

24. Ibid., 199.

25. Jonathan Elliot, *Debates in the Several States Conventions on the Adoption of the Federal Constitution*, 5 vols. (Philadelphia: Lippincott, 1907), 2:175.

26. Quoted in Richard J. Storr, "Academic Culture and the History of American Higher Education," *Journal of General Education* 5 (Oct. 1950): 13, cited in Sloan, *Education and Values*, 201.

27. Frederick Rudolph, *Curriculum: History of the American Undergraduate Course of Study since 1636* (San Francisco: Jossey-Bass, 1977), 157, cited in Sloan, *Education and Values*, 203.

28. Edward S. Conklin, "The Pedagogy of College Ethics," *Pedagogical Seminary* 18 (Dec. 1911): 427–28, cited in Sloan, *Education and Values*, 216–17.

29. Sloan, *Education and Values*, 239.

30. Ibid.

31. Ibid., 242–43.

32. Walter Lippmann, "Education vs. Western Civilization," *American Scholar* 10, no. 2 (Spring 1941): 188.

33. Chase, *Group Memory*, 132.

34. Reston, "Do Leaders Matter?"

35. John A. Howard, "Values in Private Higher Education," *Vital Speeches of the Day*, 48, no. 9 (Feb. 15, 1982): 277.

The Moral Responsibilities of Universities

10

Terrance Sandalow

IN THE YEARS SINCE the Second World War, "higher education" has emerged as one of the major influences in American life. Well over 50 percent of the age cohort now in its teens or early twenties will attend a college or university, more than a five-fold increase from the prewar period. Moreover, colleges and universities now engage in so broad a range of activities that the appellation "higher education" no longer seems entirely appropriate to describe the institutions. Community colleges, but also four-year colleges and universities, play a major role in training individuals for skilled and semiskilled occupations. Universities are our most important centers of research, and they have become so, significantly, at a time of unprecedented societal dependence on research. They are major providers of medical care. Their faculty members figure prominently as experts for government, industry, and the media; and their athletic teams are important sources of mass entertainment.

The list might be extended, but the point is clear enough. Higher education has become what in a different setting we call a "conglomerate," and a very large one at that. It employs over two

Terrance Sandalow is Edson R. Sunderland Professor of Law at The University of Michigan.

million men and women, its annual expenditures exceed $100 billion, and its total assets approach $200 billion. To be sure, the system of higher education is highly decentralized and diverse, so that it is often misleading to think of it in aggregate terms, but even individual institutions have achieved considerable size and wealth. The largest have annual budgets that exceed one billion dollars, assets totaling several times that amount, and employment rolls that number in the tens of thousands.

The question we have been asked to consider—the appropriate role of universities in forming a social morality—arises almost inevitably from the growing importance of higher education in our national life. Influence carries with it an expectation of responsibility, and an institution as influential as the American system of higher education might well be thought to have some responsibility for addressing pervasive social issues. The widespread belief that our national moral life is in need of repair thus seems to lead naturally to questions about the contribution higher education should make to the process of moral renewal.

I

Although universities are in many respects distinctive institutions, the question of their appropriate role in forming a social morality is an aspect of a larger problem that our society has not satisfactorily addressed, though it presses on us more and more insistently. How are we to think about the moral responsibility of institutions? It is a commonplace that we live in an age of large organizations, an age in which the pursuit of our goals requires collective action on a large scale. Automobiles cannot be built, nor the next generation educated, by individuals acting alone or in small groups. And so, large organizations are established to perform these and many other important functions. Yet, we lack an intellectual framework for thinking about the moral responsibilities of these organizations. Our ideas about moral responsibility have been formed in reference to individuals. Because those ideas presuppose understanding and will—distinctively human characteristics—they cannot readily be transferred to institutions. Nor is that the only difficulty. The collective exercise of power poses troublesome issues that are not raised when power is exercised by individuals. Institutions are formed to achieve limited objectives, and the authority conferred on those who direct them is circumscribed by those objectives. The attempt to ascribe moral responsibility to institutions thus raises issues of fiduciary obligation and the use of delegated power that ordinarily need not be confronted when a question is raised about the moral responsibility of individuals.

An illustration will help to reveal the difficulty of those issues. A few years ago a great national debate occurred about whether American corporations should cease doing business in South Africa. Proponents of disinvestment maintained that, by continuing to do business there, corporations were helping to maintain a brutal and racist regime. Opponents rested mainly on the contention that disinvestment would seriously harm South Africa's black population and deprive American business of whatever influence it might have in bringing about an end to apartheid. A quite different reason for opposing disinvestment is suggested by an argument Milton Friedman has made against the claim that corporations have social responsibilities beyond their obligations to shareholders to maximize profits.[1] If corporations have other social obligations, he asks, how are corporate officers to know what they are? The power the officers have been given has been conferred on the understanding that it would be employed in the interest of shareholders — not, moreover, in the latter's general interest, but in the service of their limited interest in profit maximization. No one has authorized corporate officers to decide what the public interest requires or what burdens they can justifiably impose on shareholders in promoting interests other than the latter's interest in profits.

Friedman's argument has great force, but it does not satisfactorily resolve the problem of corporate social responsibility. Most economic activity is now carried on by corporations. The consequence of accepting Friedman's argument would thus be to free the largest part of our economic life from the moral judgments that we would expect to inform and constrain the same activities if they were undertaken by individuals. Were IBM owned by an individual, no one would suppose that his decision whether or not to do business in South Africa should rest solely on an inquiry into the profitability of the activity.[2]

Yet, on Professor Friedman's argument, precisely that outcome is required if the activity is conducted by a corporation. His only response to this difficulty is to point to the power of government to prohibit economic activities that are regarded as socially undesirable. The wisdom of relying exclusively on law to mark out the limits of socially acceptable economic activity is, however, very doubtful. Individuals do not generally regard themselves as having satisfied their moral obligations merely because they have complied with the law, nor does it seem socially desirable that they should do so. The limits of what we seek to achieve by law are not coextensive with our moral ideas, in part because government lacks power to intrude into our lives in sufficient depth and in part because we do not wish it to have such power. Similar considerations argue against exclusive reliance on law to limit corporations' profit-seeking activities.

Although Professor Friedman's conclusion respecting the boundaries of corporate social responsibility is unsatisfactory, the force of his argument needs to be recognized. It too rests on moral claims. In the first instance, there is the claim of shareholders that the power they have conferred for a limited purpose should not be employed for other purposes. Ultimately, however, Friedman's argument rests on an even more fundamental moral claim, one that involves the adverse economic consequences of permitting investment in corporations only on the understanding that they may be employed to pursue whatever objectives are regarded as morally appropriate by those who control them. The considerations that incline us against Friedman's argument do not answer these claims. They merely demonstrate that the problem is more difficult than his argument recognizes. The officers of a corporation are not and should not be free to manage its affairs on the same moral principles that would guide them if the corporation were theirs, but neither should they take the law as their exclusive moral guide. It is more difficult to say what they should do. Despite the importance of corporations in our economic life, we have not yet found a satisfactory way to address that question.

Universities are not profit-making enterprises, but as they go about their activities, issues are recurrently raised that are very similar to those presented by the question of corporate social responsibility.

They too have been established for limited purposes, and the authority conferred on those who control them is limited accordingly. By what right can the latter employ that power for other purposes? And yet, it is true of universities no less than of corporations that the single-minded pursuit of the limited purposes for which they are established would free an important part of our social life from the moral judgments that should inform it. Recent history suggests the range and importance of the issues affected by this dilemma. The disinvestment question that has been so divisive an issue in many universities is nearly identical with that faced by corporations: Should a university sell its holdings in companies doing business in South Africa even though that would reduce the value of its endowment, or would doing so break faith both with donors who understood that their gifts would be used for educational purposes and with the intended beneficiaries of those gifts? Should universities accept contracts for weapons research? Are racial preferences in admission or hiring morally permissible (or morally required)? Should universities make their placement facilities available to the CIA and the Department of Defense? To employers that discriminate against homosexuals? What are the responsibilities of a college or university to its local community?

The distinctive characteristics of universities are likely to color the issues somewhat, but arguments about their moral responsibility that turn on their institutional character (as distinguished from arguments based on the nature of the enterprise) are in the main similar for universities and for corporations. There is, however, one important difference between the two that merits attention. The locus of authority is a good deal more difficult to locate in universities than in corporations. By law, the directors of a corporation are responsible for its management. The same is technically true of the trustees or regents of a university, but the social understanding is very different. Universities are expected to be, and generally are, less hierarchical and less tightly organized than corporations. Individual faculty members enjoy considerably greater freedom from institutional control than do the professional employees of corporations. A chemist employed by a pharmaceutical company is expected to engage in research that his superiors have determined to be in the best interests of the company.

Neither university trustees, nor deans, nor the faculty collectively would presume to exercise similar control over the research of a faculty member or the content of his courses. The governing principle, with relatively rare and narrow exceptions, is laissez-faire. How are we to think about the responsibility of an institution that has so little control over those who act under its auspices?

When institutional decisions are required, moreover, authority is a good deal more diffuse in universities than in corporations. Members of the faculty are technically employees, but tradition accords them a role in the governance of the institution very different from that of corporate employees. Students might conceivably be likened to the customers of a business, but the reality is plainly otherwise. They are more nearly like members of a community, entitled (in uncertain measure) to participate in its decisions. Trustees, administrators, and alumni also have claims to membership in the community and, therefore, a claim to participate in its governance. Although tradition accords different degrees of responsibility for one or another decision to one or another group, the understanding is fluid and shifting. Universities are, therefore, likely to be run more by consensus than command, a characteristic that embarrasses still further the task of ascribing responsibility to them.

Whatever difficulties we may encounter in thinking about institutional responsibility, the appropriate role of universities in forming a social morality is likely to continue as a subject of concern. The range and scale of their activities have made their behavior a matter of consequence. The decisions they make—about whom to educate, about the content and ends of education, about the proper subjects of research and the priorities among them, and about a host of other issues—have sufficient moral importance that they must be regarded as significant elements in any description of the state of our social morality. Beyond their immediate importance, moreover, the decisions taken by universities may have a significant effect on the attitudes and behavior of other institutions and of individuals. The latter will often be as important as the former, at times even more so. A university's decision about whether to disinvest in companies doing business in South Africa is not likely to have a direct effect on the plight of South Africa's blacks, but it may well help to shape a societal understanding about whether injustice in that distant place is an appropriate concern of Americans. A decision about the use of the university's placement facilities by employers that discriminate against homosexuals may or may not affect the employment opportunities of homosexual students, but it is likely to influence societal judgments about homosexuality and about whether discrimination against homosexuals is a matter of social concern.

The influence of universities on societal morality helps to explain why they have in recent years become so prominent a battleground. Groups making moral claims are likely to see the capture of universities as an important victory, gaining for them a site that is not only itself an important piece of social territory, but that also offers a staging ground for pressing their claims elsewhere. The force of their moral claims has seemed to many an adequate justification for the effort to turn the university to their purposes. Yet, there is, in E. M. Forster's phrase, a "morality of morality." The question of how moral ends should be pursued is itself an important moral question.

The difficulties that we confront in discussing the moral responsibilities of an institution are not merely impediments to a judgment about whether it can be "blamed" for an action. They are equally relevant to judgments by those within the institution about the ends toward which they may appropriately seek to direct it. The trustees of a university are no more justified than the directors of a corporation in employing its resources to promote whatever ends they would regard as morally appropriate were the resources their own. From time to time, one hears the argument that, whatever limits there may be on the rightful exercise of power by trustees, the university community as a whole should be free to employ the institution's resources toward one or another end. Just what is meant by the "community as a whole" when the "community" is as amorphous as a university is unclear, but even if that difficulty were overcome, other problems remain. Collective decision about the moral ends that the university should serve threatens the diffusion of authority characteristic of universities, a characteristic that itself rests on important moral considerations. Moreover, the members of the university community— faculty, students, trustees, donors, and whoever else may have a claim to membership—have not come together for the purpose of jointly promoting the common good. Their association in the university has more limited purposes, and it is by no means evident what warrant a majority, even a very large majority, can claim for employing the institution for other purposes.

Despite these considerations, it seems inappropriate to conclude that the members of the university community must refrain from any effort to bring its activities into line with their moral judgments. That conclusion would merely elevate the moral concerns on which it rests to a position of priority over other moral concerns with which they may at times collide. The priority of the former may at times be appropriate, but it is not evident that there is any a priori justification for concluding that they always are. A more discriminating analysis is required, one that takes account of differences among the issues that universities confront. A brief essay is not a suitable vehicle for a comprehensive analysis of those issues, but it may be useful to suggest a number of considerations that should inform the analysis.

At times, as when decisions are made about which students to admit, a university must speak with a single voice to an issue it cannot avoid, but that cannot be resolved by reference to the purposes of the institution. The university's educational responsibility sheds no light on the question of who is to be educated—whether preference in admission should be given to applicants with the greatest intellectual potential, to those who are likely to hold power in later years, or to the members of disadvantaged racial and ethnic groups. A choice must be made among these and other possibilities, and if the choice is to be morally informed, those responsible for it must attend to the relevant moral issues. There is no apparent reason that others must refrain from attempting to influence that decision.

More difficult questions are raised when an issue that must be addressed collectively involves moral concerns that arguably lie outside the province of the university. The disinvestment question offers a ready illustration. A collective decision about investment policy is inescapable, but the university's mission does not comprehend concern for all the ramifications of its decisions. The university does not exist to promote social justice, but to educate its students and to foster the advancement of knowledge. In performing the latter functions, it may well contribute to the achievement of social justice, but it does so indirectly, by enlarging the capacity of its students and by promoting the increase of knowledge. The consequence, it might be argued, is that universities may not appropriately risk the value of their endowments by refusing to invest in companies that do business in South Africa.

The difficulty with this formulation of the argument against disinvestment is that it fails to recognize the need for ethical constraints on the manner in which the university pursues its central objectives. The need for such constraints is, however, frequently and properly recognized—for example, in rules designed to protect experimental subjects even at the cost of inhibiting research that would contribute to the advancement of knowledge. Although the ethical prescription "do no harm" states too simplistic a standard, it is an appropriate reminder that we ought to concern ourselves with the harm that results from our actions. The prescription seems no less appropriate when power is exercised collectively than when it is exercised by individuals. Accordingly, if investment in companies doing business in South Africa contributes to the perpetuation of injustice, that consequence is a relevant consideration in deciding on a university investment policy.

Nevertheless, I want to suggest that disinvestment—and hence the pressure on universities to disinvest—may well be inappropriate because it employs the university's influence toward ends that are beyond the university's purview. The critical question is whether continued investment in companies doing business in South Africa actively contributes to perpetuation of the regime. If it does, as I have already argued, that consequence furnishes a legitimate, though not necessarily a decisive, reason for disinvestment. If it does not, however, disinvestment seems merely an effort to influence American public opinion toward South Africa, an aim that lies outside the purposes for which the university was established. However laudable the objective, the means chosen involves an appropriation of the university's influence. To repeat: individuals do not come together in the university for the purpose of jointly promoting the common good. Their association is for more limited purposes. To achieve those purposes, it will often be necessary to recognize that some part of the community must act in the name of the whole. But those who exercise that power—and by extension any attempt to influence them—ought to be constrained by the purposes for which it is granted. They are not free to employ the resources they control as though those resources were their own.

We have been considering situations in which an institutional decision is inescapable. In many situations, the university has another alternative: it may defer to the decisions of individuals. Many of the most important decisions in the university, especially those involving its educational and research activities, are made in that way. With some variation by discipline (and among universities), neither the educational program nor the research of the faculty is generally taken as a subject for collective decision. Although a few minimum requirements may be collectively established, the "curriculum" comprises mainly the aggregation of courses that individual faculty members wish to teach and the courses that individual students elect from the resulting smorgasbord. Collective decision about the aim and content of courses, including collectively prescribed courses, is even less likely. And even less institutional control is exercised over the faculty's research. The university thus becomes merely an environment within which individuals may pursue their individual objectives. Its institutional responsibility is taken to be only that of fostering conditions that are maximally conducive to the achievement of those objectives.

Any attempt to impose more particular responsibilities threatens that view of the university and the decision-making regime on which it rests. At my own university, for example, some faculty members and students maintain that no grant or contract for the development of weapons should be accepted. The argument rests on the claim that the university should be committed to humane values and that research that contributes to the destruction of human life is incompatible with such a commitment. If these arguments are taken to define the moral responsibility of the university, that responsibility can be met only by limiting the freedom of individual investigators. Similarly, if universities are to be held responsible for the moral development of their students, the institution—through some collective decision-making process—will have to assume greater control over the educational program.

Resistance to the idea that the university has such responsibilities is, not surprisingly, often grounded in a defense of the current diffusion of authority. For present purposes, it will be sufficient to characterize these arguments as involving a claim of academic freedom, a characterization that should bring home that the resistance also rests on a moral foundation. How the claim of academic freedom should be weighed against the claim of institutional responsibility is too large a question to be adequately addressed here, in part because it requires considerable attention to context. I want to make only one general observation: the reliance on academic freedom to avoid institutional responsibility too often ignores the extent to which the circumstances within which individual decisions are made have been created by the institution. It is only because the institution exists that a faculty member has students to teach. A faculty member's research is not only supported by institutional resources, but may also have been shaped by institutional expectations regarding research and the means by which it is to be financed. Institutional expectations regarding research may also influence decisions about the courses a faculty member wishes to teach. And students are not generally content to receive a piece of paper reciting that they have taken specified courses covering described materials. They want a degree that carries the seal of the university.

These considerations do not carry us very far in balancing the competing claims of academic freedom and institutional responsibility, but they do caution against pressing the former too hard. Some account must be taken of the fact that the decisions are made within an institution and that their consequences are in some measure affected by that circumstance. The institution cannot escape responsibility for an individual's actions simply by asserting that they are not the product of a collective decision. Some responsibility follows from its having empowered him to act or from its influence on his decision to act in the way that he has. The ethical principle that requires disinvestment if continued investment would contribute to the perpetuation of injustice seems equally to require collective safeguards against, for example, the abuse of students by faculty members. Having set a force in motion, the university is ethically bound to safeguard against harms that may result from its having done so.

II

This analysis suggests at least some limits on the role that the university should play in forming a social morality. The university does not have a roving commission to do good, nor does it have a mandate to serve as society's conscience. Whatever role it may have in forming a social morality is to be played out in the performance of its more limited responsibilities. Those responsibilities, it bears repeating, provide ample scope for significant contributions to the nation's moral life. The manner in which universities perform their responsibilities is itself an important component of our collective moral life. It is also a significant influence on the moral understanding and behavior of others. When, for example, universities illegally recruit star athletes, a lesson is taught to the young that is likely to have moral consequences far more important than the immediate consequences of the recruitment.

Despite the range and importance of their other activities, it is in the performance of their most traditional function, the education of students, that universities are likely to have the most significant impact on social morality. Yet, even when attention is directed solely to that function, the role that universities should play in forming a social morality is not an issue that one can easily imagine arising until relatively recently. As recently as fifty years ago—surely no more than seventy-five years ago—their place in the life of the nation was too peripheral for anyone to suppose that what they did would significantly affect social morality. Colleges and universities were, of course, expected to attend to the moral development of their students, but throughout the nineteenth century and well into the twentieth the percentage of the population attending institutions of higher education, even among the more influential classes, was too small for the moral life of the nation to be greatly affected by the education students received.

There are other and in many ways more interesting reasons that the question is a distinctively modern one. A century ago, it would have been assumed that a university's responsibility is to transmit morality. Now we are asked to consider the university's role in forming a social morality. Those are very different conceptions of the university's role, and it will be instructive to inquire why we should be led to consider a conception of the university's role so different from the one assumed by our grandparents and great-grandparents. An erosion of moral consensus during the past century might be thought to offer a partial explanation. Earlier generations were, on this view, bound together by a common moral understanding. Transmitting that understanding, and inculcating a commitment to it, might seem an appropriate task of education because the society knew what it believed and, therefore, what it wanted its children to believe. With the erosion of consensus there is less certainty about what should be passed on to the next generation. We are, thus, asked to consider the university's role in forming a social morality because the felt need now is for a consensus to be forged from the current welter of moral understandings and commitments.

The problem with this explanation lies in the difficulty of assessing the differences between our own and an earlier time. We are acutely aware of the moral disagreements in our own time, but just as mountain peaks seem to flatten out as they recede, the controversies of an earlier time lose significance for us as our distance from them increases. Additional difficulties are posed by the necessity of gauging not merely the intensity of moral controversies in different periods, but the relative importance of the controversies in the overall social fabric. The question of whether there is less moral consensus now than fifty or a hundred years ago is, therefore, a complex historical problem that does not admit of answers as simple as those served up by nostalgia for a dimly perceived past.

The period to which nostalgia tends to be directed is the latter half of the nineteenth and the early years of the current century. Whether moral consensus was or was not greater then than now, that time differed from our own in a number of ways relevant to the question of why universities in the earlier period might be taken to have responsibility for transmitting morality while it now seems appropriate to ask about their role in forming a social morality. Both the student bodies and the faculties of colleges and universities were a good deal more homogeneous then than now. The composition of both was restricted by race, ethnic group, class, religion, and sex. Homogeneity was enhanced by the local character of all institutions and by the sectarian affiliation of many of them. Whatever differences there may have been in the larger society were, accordingly, considerably softened by the similarity of background and resulting similarity of outlook among the members of a particular college or university community. The notion that universities are charged with transmitting morality to the next generation fits much more easily into such an environment than it fits into the vastly different setting of contemporary higher education.

Changing conceptions of morality have also played a part in altering ideas about the university's role. A century ago, morality was more likely than at present to be thought of as rooted in an external, generally a religious, source. Contemporary notions about morality are more likely to regard it as a human construct. The idea that education consists, at least in part, of transmitting morality to students does not comport well with the latter conception of morality. If morality is a human construct, the prevailing understanding of it is always open to question, far more so than if it is thought to be rooted in an external source. Attention is thus directed away from the transmission of morality toward questions about the wisdom of what has been constructed. The salience of those questions leads to uncertainty and controversy about what is to be transmitted.

The idea that education ought to be concerned with transmitting moral values nonetheless persists and forms the basis for a good deal of current criticism of universities. The goals of an educational program must, however, take some account of social circumstances, and it is a fair question whether the goals of the critics adequately take account of the circumstances of our society.

The contemporary conception of morality as a human construct is reinforced by a contemporary tendency to regard prevailing social and economic structures as a subject of choice. Increasingly, those structures are not considered fixed, defining boundaries within which individual decisions must be made, but are themselves thought of as created by humans and, therefore, alterable by them. The ethic of individual responsibility that universities sought to transmit to students in the nineteenth and early twentieth centuries does not fit comfortably into this intellectual framework. The reason is not that issues of personal responsibility no longer seem important to us, but that they have come to seem less important than issues of social and economic organization. The latter are no less moral issues than the former, but they are also political issues. At stake in the controversies over their resolution is the distribution of status, wealth, and power. Universities cannot undertake to transmit "answers" to most such issues if for no other reason than because our society has none to offer. In the absence of consensus and with the loss of faith in an external source of moral judgment, any effort by universities to inculcate their students with "answers" will seem merely a partisan response.

The political character of the moral issues made salient by contemporary ways of thinking about morality is, however, only one of the difficulties that a contemporary university would face were it to view its task as that of transmitting morality to its students. Earlier, I contrasted an older conception of morality, one resting on external sources and emphasizing an ethic of individual responsibility, with a modern conception that regards morality as a human construct and that gives more emphasis to social and economic institutions than to individual responsibility. But the characterization of the former as "older" does not mean that it is no longer current. Contemporary Americans tend to hold both conceptions simultaneously, though the extent to which reliance is placed on one or the other differs widely in different parts of the population.

The belief is widespread that universities have failed to attend adequately to the moral development of their students, but one consequence of the moral divisions among us is disagreement about just where universities have failed. At the risk of caricature, the critics may be divided into two main camps: a "conservative" camp that deplores mainly the failure of universities to instill students with an ethic of individual responsibility, and a "liberal" camp that is primarily critical of the universities' failure to inculcate a commitment to work toward social changes that will remedy various social and economic ills. The use of political labels to describe moral and educational positions seems appropriate in this instance because, perhaps not surprisingly, there is some correspondence between each camp's political agenda and what it perceives as the failing of higher education.

Drug use, violence, a lack of respect for authority, and declining standards of honesty and sexual morality rank high on the conservatives' list of pressing social problems. All are attributed in some measure to the failure of universities and other educational institutions to aid their students in developing an appropriate set of personal values. Not all of these problems are regarded as such by liberals, but even when they are, the remedies offered by liberals are likely to be quite different from those proposed by conservatives. The remedy proposed by the latter is implicit in their views about the source of the problems: universities should lead their students to an understanding of the importance of certain personal values, an understanding that would, if generally held, almost definitionally eliminate the problems. Liberals are more likely to attribute the problems to very different causes and, as a consequence, to offer very different remedies. Violence, they are likely to believe, is rooted in poverty and dishonesty among students attributable to the overwhelming pressure of current educational practices. The remedy, thus, is to eliminate poverty and reduce the pressure on students. The frequency of that response is itself likely to be taken by conservatives as a symptom of moral decay and probably also as a cause of it.

In any event, the liberal critics of higher education regard racism, pollution, the persistence of poverty, and the threat of war as far more serious moral problems than those emphasized by conservatives. Just as the conservative critics tend to look back with nostalgia to the nineteenth century, the liberal critics also have fond memories of a "golden age"—in their case the 1960s. The moral development at which education should aim, in their view, is an awakening of the remembered spirit of that time in each generation of students. Conservatives tend to reject that view on the ground that it politicizes the educational process, an objection that liberals counter with the assertion that the quiescence produced by an ethic of individual responsibility is no less political. An education that emphasizes that ethic, the latter maintain, diverts attention from the most serious moral problems that our society confronts; worse, it leads students to hold individuals responsible for problems that are socially created and can be addressed only by an acceptance of social responsibility.

Although they are admittedly caricatures, these broad-brush descriptions suggest the difficulties that the contemporary university would encounter were it to adopt either view. The moral development at which each camp aims is a stance toward life. A university cannot inculcate the attitudes and values that either regards as appropriate merely by requiring students to register for a prescribed course, as it might if the task were only to assure that every graduate understands trigonometry or is acquainted with a set of ethical precepts. If the university is to be held responsible for the moral development of students, as moral development is understood by both conservative and liberal critics, a pervasive commitment to that end will be required. Moral values permeate the curriculum — indeed, all of the relationships that the university has with its students. To discharge its responsibility, the university would be required to act collectively to assure that appropriate use is made of all the opportunities thus presented.

Collective decision would also be required about the moral views to be instilled in students. By whom is that decision to be made? In a relatively few institutions, generally those with close ties to a religious denomination, the question is not very difficult. Hierarchical relationships within the denomination or the shared moral perspectives of students and faculty furnish a sufficient answer. For most universities, the question will be more difficult, perhaps unanswerable. Their faculties, which traditionally have borne responsibility for the educational program, are as riven by moral differences as the general population. Those differences can be accommodated within the prevailing regime of laissez-faire, but that solution is ruled out by a conception of education that calls for inculcating prescribed values. Perhaps one need not be too concerned about the divisions within faculties, because it seems unlikely that their authority would continue for very long if they openly sought to inculcate collectively prescribed moral views. Public acceptance of faculty authority over the educational program rests in part on a belief in the faculty's expertise. There is little reason to suppose that the public regards the faculty as having a special competence with respect to the great moral issues that confront the nation. Of course, sophisticated members of the public appreciate that moral ideas infuse much of what is taught in universities, but it is one thing to tolerate the freedom of the faculty when students are exposed to a multitude of voices, no one of which is taken to be authoritative, and quite another to do so when the university speaks with a single voice.

One may doubt also whether universities are capable of achieving the goals of those who look to them to provide moral guidance to students. At its best, higher education is a powerful experience — at times even a transforming one — greatly enhancing the capacities of students and opening them to wholly new possibilities in thinking about ways to live a life. It is, nonetheless, only one influence among many, and it is likely to be least influential in shaping the values of students. Sectarian institutions that draw their student bodies primarily from a narrow population that share a common outlook must, once again, be sharply distinguished from other colleges and universities. The former, like nineteenth-century institutions, are called upon to reinforce values that hold sway in the community from which their students come and to which they will return. The student bodies of most institutions, by contrast, are drawn from diverse backgrounds, and they anticipate lives in a world characterized by a diversity of values and ethical practices. The connotations of the phrase "ivory tower" suggest the limited influence of the university when it seeks to impart values that diverge very markedly from those that students perceive in the outside world.

In recent years, for example, the organized bar has expressed considerable concern about the ethical behavior of lawyers and their commitment to professional ideals. The concerns expressed range over a broad area, from the frequency of dishonesty and lawbreaking by lawyers to an asserted failure of many lawyers to meet their public responsibilities. Among the issues raised are some that are highly controversial, such as the appropriate balance between zealous pursuit of a client's goals and recognition of public and other interests that may conflict with those goals. The most tangible consequences of the bar's avowed concern are a requirement that law schools require their students to take a course in professional responsibility and an admonition to faculties to emphasize ethical issues throughout the curriculum. It is, however, naive to suppose that a course — or even three years of legal education — will have a decisive influence on the behavior of most law school graduates. Even if law faculties were of one mind regarding the issues – a wildly improbable supposition – too many other factors are at work that overpower whatever influence three years of legal education may have.

Students come to law schools as adults. They are a good deal less malleable than seems to be supposed by those who look to legal education to solve the ethical problems of the profession. To be sure, the determinants of lawyer behavior are not irrevocably fixed prior to the first day of law school, but to the extent that the personal characteristics, attitudes, and values of fledgling lawyers are still being shaped, lessons learned in law school about the appropriate behavior of lawyers are, for nearly all students, likely to be much less influential than what they learn from observing the behavior of practicing lawyers. It should not be surprising that the lawyers encountered in summer clerkships and in the early years of practice are the models to whom students and young lawyers look for clues about how they ought to conduct themselves. After all, it is those lawyers, not the members of law faculties, who face the questions that students and young lawyers confront in practice and who lead the lives to which the latter aspire.

III

The hopes of both conservative and liberal critics misconceive the aims of higher education and its potential. A pluralist society cannot accommodate a conception of education that calls for inculcating controversial moral values.[3] It does not follow that universities have no role in the moral development of their students. In the remainder of this essay, I want to sketch briefly some ideas about the contribution universities can make.

At one time, there would have been widespread agreement that, as Herbert Spencer put it, "education has for its object the formation of character."[4] In the sense that Spencer employed it, the word "character" is not heard very often these days. So used, it is less likely to inspire than to evoke a faint smile. The loss of meaning is regrettable, for the word captured an aggregation of qualities that are highly useful in sustaining a life. A man or woman of character has a moral code, but he or she also has something more: the personal strengths that are necessary to steadfastness of purpose in the face of life's vicissitudes. Disappointment, embarrassment, boredom, fear, pain, and temptation are obstacles to the attainment of our goals. They are also part of the common experience of mankind. Courage, patience, perseverance, and other qualities that enable us to overcome these impediments are, for that reason, universally regarded as virtues, and since they are necessary to the success of any sustained moral undertaking, their enhancement is a central element of moral development.

Developing these virtues is a traditional aim of education, one that deserves greater emphasis than it currently receives in higher education. Colleges and universities are not, to be sure, positioned to play a decisive role in the formation of their students' characters. Students come to them as adults or near-adults. The faculty-student ratio and other demands on the faculty's time tend to preclude a level of personal contact that might permit faculty members to become an important personal influence in the lives of their students. Still, the limited potential of higher education for influencing the development of character does not justify a conclusion that it is irrelevant to that development. Character traits like those we are considering are, as Joseph Schwab has written, "enhanced only by undertaking and sustaining the actions pertaining to [them] to the point of perceiving and enjoying the enhanced competence which results."[5] By availing themselves of the opportunities they have for leading students to such actions, universities can strengthen those traits. The opposite is also true. Inappropriate behavior can help to weaken them.

Several years ago, in a talk concerned with issues in legal education, I urged that faculty inattention to class attendance, preparedness for class, timely submission of papers, and the like represented missed opportunities for assisting students to develop desirable character traits and, worse, probably contributed to their erosion.[6] The following day, a privately published newsletter carried a prominent faculty member's critical account of the talk under the headline "Sandalow Calls For Repression." The lesson, I suppose, is that we live in a time in which every objective may be regarded as political. Nevertheless, the virtues I have been considering are not very controversial, and the effort to develop them does not threaten pluralist values. They are not only compatible with but necessary to widely differing visions of moral responsibility.

In any event, the university's greatest potential for influencing the moral development of students is in the contribution that it can make to their intellectual development. Moral judgments are not purely matters of taste, about which individuals differ as they do when one prefers tomatoes and another prefers carrots. They depend on knowledge and disciplined thought. Although formal education is but one influence among many affecting character development, it is in our society the chief instrument of intellectual development.

Universities thus play an important role in the moral development of students when they assist the latter in developing the capacity to think clearly, to identify and articulate premises, and to develop arguments that flow in an orderly fashion from those premises. Enhancing the ability of students to read, similarly, contributes significantly to their capacity for informed moral judgment. The ability to capture meaning from the printed word and to understand the possibilities and uses of fixity, vagueness, ambiguity, and change in language is essential to participation in a community of thought that extends beyond very narrow boundaries of space and time, boundaries that would otherwise confine moral judgment within personal experience. Moral judgment is also aided by a number of intellectual virtues whose development is a central task of higher education. These virtues are best described negatively, as freedom from common hazards to clear thought—hazards such as self-interest, provincialism of time and place, overdependence on familiar categories of thought, sentimentality, and an inability to tolerate uncertainty.

Informed moral judgment also depends on knowledge. At the most elementary level, students need to develop an understanding of the crucial role of facts in moral judgments. Facts are, however, all around us, and their significance is not generally self-evident. Some comprehension is also required of the theories that men have developed in an effort to apprehend the world around them. An informed moral judgment may, thus, depend on familiarity with economics, biology, or any of the other social or natural sciences. In acquainting its students with those subjects the university makes an important contribution to their moral development. The capacity for informed moral judgment is, finally, enhanced by familiarity with the ideas that others have had about moral issues. The study of ethics, literature, law, and other humanistic disciplines, is, therefore, also important to the moral development of students, not as instruction in morality, but in enlarging the range of ideas available to students in thinking about moral issues.

The university thus contributes to the moral development of students even when it seems inattentive to that objective. In attending to their intellectual development, it contributes also to their moral development by enhancing their capacity to make moral judgments. That is not an inconsiderable contribution. My experience may be atypical, but the young people I have known during a quarter-century as a member of a university faculty have not, in the main, been morally indifferent. It is tempting to say, rather, that too many have suffered from a surfeit of morality. The real problem, however, is not an excess of moral commitment, but the superficiality of their moral judgments, their intensity of feeling about issues they have barely considered. They are deeply sensitive to moral issues, but their education too often seems to have left them ill equipped to judge those issues, at times even unaware of what is involved in making a moral judgment. A strengthening of the university's educational program to overcome these deficiencies would make a far more important contribution to the moral development of these young people and to our collective moral life than any effort to inculcate students with a particular conception of morality.

Notes

1. Milton Friedman, *Capitalism and Freedom* (Chicago: University of Chicago Press, 1962), 133–36.

2. Professor Friedman at points does employ arguments—as when he relies on the social interests served by profit maximization—that suggest that individuals also are obligated to be profit maximizers as long as they remain within the bounds set by law. I have not interpreted the argument that way because of the implausibility of such a position. So construed, for example, the argument would require a restaurant owner, in the absence of civil rights legislation, to deny service to blacks if doing so would maximize the profits of the enterprise.

3. The point is somewhat overstated. A pluralist society can accommodate, and is very likely enriched by, the existence of some institutions devoted to precisely that conception of education. It could not, however, accommodate a system of higher education in which that conception is predominant.

4. Herbert Spencer, *Social Statics* (New York: D. Appleton, 1865), 201.

5. Terrance Sandalow, "The Moral Responsibility of Law Schools," *Journal of Legal Education* 34 (1984): 163.

6. Joseph J. Schwab, *College Curriculum and Student Protest* (Chicago: University of Chicago Press, 1969), 285.

Index